A WELSH ODYSSEY:
IN THE FOOTSTEPS OF GERALD OF WALES

A WELSH ODYSSEY:
in the footsteps of Gerald of Wales

Michael Curig Roberts

Gwasg Carreg Gwalch

First published in 2011

© Michael Curig Roberts

© Gwasg Carreg Gwalch

Published with the financial support of the
Welsh Book Council

ISBN: 978-1-84527-345-5

Cover design: Siôn Ilar
Line drawings: Gillian Docker Tillotson

Published by Gwasg Carreg Gwalch,
12 Iard yr Orsaf, Llanrwst, Wales LL26 0EH
tel: 01492 642031
fax: 01492 641502
email: books@carreg-gwalch.com
website: www.carreg-gwalch.com

Contents

ANGLESEY

Rhuddlan
Conwy
Bangor
Caernarfon
St.Asaph
Basingwerk
Chester
Whitchurch
Oswestry
Shrewsbury

Nefyn
BARDSEY
ISLAND
Llanfair
Tywyn
Llanbadarn Fawr
Strata Florida
Bromfield
Ludlow

New Radnor
Cruker
Leominster
Hereford

St Dogmaels
Cardigan
Llanddewi
Brefi
Lampeter
Nevern
Llanddew
Hay-on-Wye
St.David's
Camrose
Carmarthen
Brecon
Monmouth
Abergavenny
Haverfordwest
Whitland
Cydweli
Usk
Caerleon
Swansea
Margam
Llandaff
Newport
Ewenny
Cardiff
The Journey
BARRY
ISLAND

6

Acknowledgements

I acknowledge most gratefully the many who have assisted and encouraged me in writing this book and who have supported me in my search and travels around Wales.

I would like to thank Gillian Docker Tillotson for all her illustrations, and for her continual support and inspiration to me throughout my journey.

My family, Philippa, William and Elizabeth, all had belief in my ability to achieve this project and gave me the advantage of their many helpful criticisms and suggestions.

On my travels I met many generous people whose names are too numerous to mention, who gave me their time and shared their local knowledge and experience with me, pointing out many matters of interest which would otherwise have eluded me. Also I would like to thank the numerous named and unnamed local historians and enthusiasts who have so lovingly written about their churches, castles, buildings and histories; these have proved invaluable.

In particular, I thank Jen Llywelyn for her tireless editing and advice; Eurwyn Wiliam for his preface; the Welsh Books Council for supporting this publication with a grant; and Gwasg Carreg Gwalch for having the courage to support this my first literary venture.

Finally, I would like to thank Gerald himself who, through his writings from centuries ago, inspired me so many years later to retrace his steps.

Preface

This book follows in the footsteps of a seven-week recruiting drive through Wales made by Archbishop Baldwin of Canterbury in 1188, based on a contemporaneous record of the journey by one of his travelling companions. Apart from the light it throws on how men were recruited for the Crusades, the event is of particular importance to us in Wales because it was the first journey through the whole country that was recorded in detail until the Duke of Beaufort's progress in the seventeenth century.

But what makes the work even more interesting is the character and interests of its author. The three-quarters Norman but quarter-Welsh and Welsh-speaking Gerald de Barri (Gerald of Wales, *Gerallt Gymro*) was deeply interested not only in what he saw but also what he heard about the people and the regions that he journeyed through. Indeed, as the most important contemporary chronicler of our early beliefs and credos, Gerald is the founding father of the study of Welsh folklore and folk customs. As the earliest recorder of such traditions in the field he was also one of the world's earliest social anthropologists.

Although the earliest roots of the Mabinogion cycle are considerably older, Gerald was the first author to put on paper the myths and legends of the Welsh people; and although his factual accuracy has been rightly challenged (such as the assertion that the Welsh were essentially a pastoral people), nevertheless his work remained the basis for much of Welsh historiography until the nineteenth century, and is still a seminal text for understanding ourselves as a people. It is the earliest rounded reflection of our hopes, fears and aspirations. Perhaps sadly, some of the national traits that Gerald first identified, such as divisiveness and hospitality (like the tendency in Welsh-speaking communities to turn too readily to English, thus obviating the need for incomers to make any effort to learn the historical first language of the country), still serve to make us easy prey for our more assertive and more numerous neighbours.

I hope that this thoroughly accessible book will encourage others to turn to Gerald's texts – excellent English and Welsh translations exist of both the *Itinerary* and *Description of Wales* – and indeed to interest themselves more in the history of Wales's topography, and to appreciate how tales and beliefs about it, such as were recounted so vividly by Gerald, are crucial to its understanding.

Eurwyn Wiliam
Emeritus Keeper and sometime Director,
National History Musem, St. Fagans
February 2011

Introduction

In 1188 Giraldus Cambrensis (Gerald de Barri, or Gerald of Wales, as he is known in English; Gerallt Gymro in Welsh), set out with the Archbishop of Canterbury, Baldwin, to travel around the whole of Wales, recruiting men to 'take the cross' and join the Third Crusade to the Holy Land planned by Pope Innocent III.

Gerald was forty-two, a canon of St David's and Archdeacon of Brecon, and in 1175 he had been elected by the canons of St David's as bishop of the see – only to be turned down by Henry II. The king regarded him as a man of great honesty and ability but feared that, because of his ancestry, his appointment would strengthen the Welsh against the English and thus against Henry's own power.

Gerald's father, Sir William de Barri, was a Norman knight; his mother, Angharad, was Welsh. Her parents were Princess Nest (daughter of Rhys ap Tewdr (d.1093)) and the Norman lord, Gerald of Windsor. Although Gerald de Barri was thus of dual nationality, it is as a Welshman that he saw himself and is renowned (hence the name Gerallt Gymro, which honours his Welshness and the fact that he spoke Welsh). Indeed, in one of his submissions to Pope Innocent III to be Bishop of Wales, Gerald asks:

> Because I am a Welshman am I to be debarred from all preferments in Wales? On the same reasoning so would an Englishman in England, a Frenchman in France, an Italian in Italy. But I am sprung from the Princes of Wales and the Barons of the Marches, and when I see injustice in either race I hate it.

His life was dedicated to Wales and to the enhancement of

the church in Wales. Despite this he was still useful to Henry II in many ways, and thus in 1188 he was specifically requested by the king to undertake helping the English Archbishop Baldwin to muster Welsh soldiers for the Third Crusade.

The Second Crusade had been disastrous. Saladin had recovered Jerusalem for Islam on 2 October 1187, and the highly important relic of the True Cross was lost to Christendom. It was hoped that the Third Crusade would put all this to rights.

'Taking the cross' entailed marking a man's clothing with a cloth cross, often given to him by a member of the clergy, which he would then wear always on his dress. This showed that he had entered into a commitment or contract with God to join the Crusade to liberate the Holy Land – and in particular, Jerusalem – from the 'infidels' and Saracens. In accepting the cross he was signing on for a journey of some 2,500 miles, to be covered on the sea, on horseback, and probably on foot if he only had one horse and it were to die on the journey (which was far from unusual). Men of peasant stock would be foot soldiers. But for all those going it would have been a huge adventure – for many, the greatest adventure of their lives. The time away from home would have been contractually two years, but in fact would have been considerably longer. The likelihood of death by disease or starvation, let alone from battle, was huge: it has been estimated that up to 50 per cent of men joining in the Second Crusade died this way rather than from actual fighting. On the other hand, the prospect of death was softened by the promise of martyrdom and a guaranteed place in paradise, with the remission of all sins. This has resonance with the present interpretation by some of Islamic Jihad, and after all, the Crusades were regarded by the Popes of the day as 'holy wars'.

Also there was the possibility, not often achieved, of obtaining great wealth through booty after a successful battle. The church fully accepted the concept of temporal wealth as well as spiritual benefit – as long as the booty taken was not too great, as otherwise the sin of greed would detract from spiritual and other benefits.

The emotional or actual cost of going on a Crusade was considerable. Although some women and wives did go on the Crusades, the vast majority were left behind to all the temptations arising from the absence of their loved ones, and the pressures on family lives were very real. For example, Rhys ap Gruffudd was determined to take the cross, but when he returned home his wife 'by female artifices diverted him wholly from his noble purpose'.

Given the huge influence at the time of chivalric concepts and religious fervour, another young man, when he took the cross, is stated as having said 'What man of spirit can refuse to undertake this journey, since among all imaginable inconveniences, nothing worse can happen to anyone than return'.

Once the cross had been taken one was bound by the oath, and there was no escape unless one was given absolution by the Pope from the vow. This absolution was usually given so that the individual could carry on other more important services for the Papacy. Gerald, as we will see, was one of the first of some 3,000 men to take the cross. It was important for clergymen to go on the Crusade, at the very least to act as cheerleaders for the rest. He set out, sailing to France in 1189, but he was sent back to England by King Richard I, on Archbishop Baldwin's advice, and was given absolution from his vow to go on the Crusade by the Cardinal Legate, John of Anagni. As for Baldwin, he travelled on to the Holy Land and died in November 1190, possibly a victim of 'a particularly dreadful plague [which] hit the camp besieging Acre in 1190–1 and thousands perished, both rich and poor alike' (Phillips).

Gerald's journey around Wales was carried out in the amazing time of seven weeks. Apart from the travel, which must of itself have been very onerous, Gerald, Baldwin and others preached as they went, gaining the support of the Welsh princes to their cause. Gerald, in *Itinerarium Cambriae* (*The Journey through Wales*), records all the activities of the seven weeks, almost in diary form. He also records many historical, mythical and contemporary stories and occurrences during the expedition. Though Gerald was a Welsh-speaker, he wrote in Latin.

The Journey through Wales has been translated several times, the first published in London in 1585. The 1978 translation by Professor Lewis Thorpe initially interested me in Gerald; subsequent research took me to the 1806 translation by the archaeologist and antiquarian Sir Richard Colt Hoare, who was descended from the founder of C. Hoare & Co's bank, and had inherited the Stourhead estate from his grandfather. After the death of his wife and their second child in 1785, Sir Richard, 'to ameliorate my mind', took to travel throughout Europe. Then, when travel became difficult around the time of the French Revolution, he resorted to travel in Britain, developing a special fondness for Wales. He even bought a cottage near Bala. In the summer of 1802 he took as his objective 'to follow the interesting and highly curious itinerary of Giraldus Cambrensis through north and south Wales in the year 1188, and make a collection of drawings to illustrate it'. He later translated both parts of Gerald's description of the journey. It is from Hoare's work that I have drawn substantially. As Hoare had been on Gerald's journey (which Thorpe had not), and had, as it were, seen the sights, it seemed to me that he would bring Gerald's journey more to life. I have also quoted from other writers and explorers of Wales at the turn of the nineteenth century.

My purpose is not to write a learned dissertation into the history of Gerald, despite the fact that he was an exceptionally interesting man. What was of interest to me was how, in those times, Gerald and Archbishop Baldwin, together with what must have been a large entourage, managed to traverse the whole of Wales, a distance of some 900 miles, in such a short time, and the adventure, for want of a better word, that they undertook. It seemed to me to be a challenge to see if it was still possible to follow their path in the twenty-first century. I wanted to see what they might have seen, to see what remains from their day, and to discover other areas of interest which have been created or have changed since their day and which might have appealed to Gerald's imagination had he lived in our age.

What we know of Gerald's character is based mainly on his own evidence in his books. He was clearly very charismatic and ambitious, and was well-versed, and indeed well-placed, in both spiritual and temporal politics at the end of the twelfth century. He was a storyteller par excellence, a writer with sixteen known texts to his score, and a cartographer. He would have been a good companion on the road. He was clearly someone of pleasant character and this part of his nature shines through his writing. Sadly his life was to end, as we shall see, without his ambition of being Archbishop of St David's being realised. He died a disappointed man – though not, it would seem, an embittered one.

I also wanted to relate some of the stories Gerald told, and consider the plausibility of some of them: for example, the floating islands, and the one-eyed fish of Snowdonia. Finally, as a self-indulgence, I wanted to revisit the 'Land of my Fathers', particularly Capel Curig and around

Caernarfon and Bangor in north Wales, and to rekindle some memories of my early life.

So this book is not a history nor a travel book, but I hope it will inspire others to look at various areas in Wales from a different perspective, both through the eyes of the Middle Ages (which were far from dark), and to enjoy with Gerald and Archbishop Baldwin the countryside, the folklore, the ancient ruins, and the myths of Wales, with a little of the modern added.

The route taken by Gerald and Baldwin is set out fairly clearly by Gerald in his 'Journey'. They set out soon after Ash Wednesday (2 March), probably on 4 March, from Hereford, arriving back at Hereford some seven weeks later on 23 April. During their journey the party stayed, in addition to castles, at various religious houses of various denominations. It is helpful to see how these had developed into the form they had. For example the Benedictine monasteries were largely close to large towns whereas the Cistercians were in the depths of the country. Initially the rule of St Benedict (541) was adopted by all monks: the essential features of it were prayer, labour, silence, a common life and common property. But among the early Benedictines each monastery was independent and self-governing. The result was that in the course of time the discipline and life of the monasteries varied infinitely: and there was no co-operation for self-defence among the various monasteries. So in the tenth century the Cluniac order was formed. This was the first attempt at organisation. The Abbot of Clugny (Cluny) became head of a vast number of monasteries in different countries of Europe and the priors of each one owed allegiance to him. They were appointed by him and paid revenues to the head abbey and the general fund of the Order. This organisation was monarchical, even despotic, and in effect, the Abbot of

Clugny was the pope of monasticism. The movement acquired enormous influence in the church as a whole, getting control of the papacy, insisting that the church should be independent of the state, and that the celibacy of the clergy should be practically enforced. But the Cluniacs, instead of withdrawing from the world, began to dominate it, losing many of the essential features of monasticism.

Another reform movement arose in about 1100: the formation of the Cistercian Order. This aimed at reviving the Benedictine rule in all its strictness, insisting especially on manual labour. Cistercian houses were founded in desolate places, as far removed from populous centres as possible. But the Order differed from the early Benedictines in that each Cistercian house was independent and self-governing, electing its own abbot. However, all abbots would come together at stated times for general assemblies or chapters, and these general assemblies were the supreme governing body in the Order. Thus unity was established, and the organisation was close, but not monarchical, in a great federation. The Cistercians tended to side with local politics and leaders.

At the time of the Crusades there was a further refinement. The military order combined the life of a monk with that of a soldier. The Regular or Augustinian Canons combined the life of a monk with the life of a parish priest. And this ideal – new to the Middle Ages – received its highest realisation in the Dominican (the 'black friars'), the Franciscan friars (the 'grey friars'), and the Carmelites (the 'white friars'), shortly after Gerald's time. Originally a monk left the world in order to become religious whereas the friar aimed at making the world religious. The monk's main object was to save his own soul, but the friar's was to save the souls of others. Despite their differences the various orders continued to flourish in Britain until the Dissolution under

Henry VIII, and still exist throughout the world.

Apart from the actual journeying, the logistics of the trip must have been pretty onerous, even though they were being routinely entertained, one assumes, along the way. Gerald must have been fairly instrumental in the planning, especially with his dual nationality, being both Welsh and Norman.

Gerald appears to have known well all the princes in the three kingdoms of Wales, Deheubarth, Gwynedd and Powys, and he and his party would be welcomed in each area by the various princes who conducted them through their various areas of control. Even so, we are told that Archbishop Baldwin, when facing the journey north into Gwynedd, 'was too frightened to cross the Dyfi into territory that no Norman could safely go'. Equally the canons of St David's had tried to stop the Archbishop's visit. Wales was and had been a volatile place, and was again to revert to warfare not long after the journey, so they must have been fearful of the mission and the outcome. In the event, on the whole everything worked almost like clockwork during the seven weeks they were together, and the mission appears to have been a success.

Inevitably some of Gerald's route around Wales has changed and, at times, I have followed modern roads, rather than difficult paths only passable on foot or on horseback. In Gerald's day the roads, by modern standards, would have been at best rutted and difficult. The Roman roads still existed but it is unlikely that their paving did. Otherwise the 'roads' would have been cart tracks at best, or overgrown pathways at worst. There were no maps, so inland one had to get to the next village or hamlet by memory or local guidance. Their journey around the coast would have been easier to follow. Where I have wandered from Gerald's route, I have researched the more obscure paths from other explorers, mainly recorded in the nineteenth century.

Nevertheless my primary purpose in retracing the footsteps of Gerald Cambrensis and Archbishop Baldwin, over 850 years ago, has been achieved. It has revealed to me a wealth of Welsh history, and enabled me to recall and relive the outstanding beauty of the modern Welsh coastline and countryside and to appreciate from a modern perspective the historic and contemporary treasure which is Wales.

Michael Curig Roberts
June 2011

Chapter 1
The journey through Hereford and Radnor

On Friday March 4 Gerald set out on his journey around Wales with Baldwin, Archbishop of Canterbury. Gerald himself refers to the 'great number of terrible disasters which, as a result of the miserable desire to seize possession of land, have occurred in our time'. Thomas à Becket, Baldwin's predecessor but one as Archbishop of Canterbury, had been murdered only eighteen years before, and the political effect of that action must have been very much in the minds of the travellers. There had been unrest in Wales as recently as two years before their journey in 1186:

> At this time Cadwalader sonne to the Lord Rhees was slaine privilie in West Wales, and buried in Ty Gwyn. The next yeare Owen Vachan, the sonne of Madoc ap Meredyth, was slaine in the castle of Carreghira in the night time, by Gwynwynwyn and Cadwalhon, the sonnes of Owen Cyreliog, and shortlie after Llewelyn sonne to Cadwallan ap Gruffyth ap Conan, who was smothered by the Englishman, was taken by his own brethren, and had his eyes put out.
>
> (Welsh Chronicle by Dr Powel)

Gerald does not record who or how many were in the party, but the number must have been considerable if only to safeguard the travellers in what were very uncertain times. Taking into account the various individuals mentioned by Gerald, the party could not have been less than fifty in number. There were, at the least, Baldwin and Gerald, Peter de Leia, Bishop of St David's, and no doubt a number of accompanying clergy. Ranulphus de Glanville, the Chief Judiciary and member of the King's Privy Council, was also in attendance as they set out, and they must have had sufficient soldiers and retinue for their protection. Whilst they were entertained during the journey there must also have been horses carrying luggage and servants, and grooms as well as others in support. The important members of the group would have been on horses, but, no doubt, many of the support staff would have been on foot. The size of the group makes it even more of a feat to have travelled all around the coast of Wales in seven weeks. Even with modern horse-power it is a daunting task.

It must be recalled that the Archbishop had already journeyed from Canterbury to Hereford and his progression would have been very gruelling including, presumably, preaching along the way. We do not know how long that first part of his expedition took but it must have been at least a week. For Gerald the trek from Brecon would not have been quite so strenuous.

Inevitably some of the paths Gerald and Baldwin and their party trod cannot be followed by car and some must be conjectural given modern roads and paths, but most of their route is reasonably clear. For example, it is a reasonable assumption that they set out from Hereford on the old Roman road alongside the Wye, now the A438. The weather may have added to the hazards of the road (though it is thought that the weather was better in those days). 'The seasons were predictable. Planting began in April, and the months of June, July and August were reliably warm and settled. Average summer temperatures were 0.7–1.0 degree Celsius warmer than they are today. Harvests were dependable and winters mild.' (Crane). However, there probably would have been plenty of rain and perhaps the magnificent peaks of Snowdonia would still have been covered with snow and not have been made invisible in the cloud and mists. Gerald does not refer to seeing snow and ice in his travels but must from time to time, as he journeyed north, have seen the magnificence of Snowdonia, to which he refers as Eryri (the haunt of the eagles).

Initially Gerald and Baldwin would have spent some time in Hereford recovering from their prior journeys and preparing for their future expedition. Parts of the town would still be recognisable to them today. The present cathedral, in all its glory, is, of course, a far cry from that of 1188, the building having been augmented over the years, and even now it is constantly changing.

By 1188 the original nave had been built, as had the south transept, but the nave Gerald knew would have been much darker than nowadays as the middle row of arches has been enlarged. The top row of arches in the clerestory, in his time, would have had much smaller windows. The changes to the present windows came some 200 years later, as did further alterations that would have occurred after the dramatic collapse of the tower and the nave in 1786. However, the south transept is very much the same as when it was built in about 1130 and the size of the cathedral nave would not have been very different.

If Gerald visited today he would no doubt recognise the font, which is possibly the oldest artefact in the cathedral, with carved apostles covering its surrounds and much of the infrastructure. One can almost feel his spirit as he contemplated the difficult and challenging road ahead, the constant companionship of the Archbishop, and the uncertainty of the welcome they might receive from the princes of Wales. He must have feared for the comfort and hospitality they would receive during their journey, as a fair number of the clergy were not impressed that an Archbishop of Canterbury was straying into the territory and the area of influence of the Welsh church. Whilst everyone was Catholic, church politics and rivalry could, as we will see, enter into the warmth or otherwise of the greeting of the clergy. In particular this applied to the canons of St David's, who tried to stop the journey happening. Gerald himself seems to have entirely put on hold for the duration of his journey with Baldwin his personal ambition to head the Church of Wales. Nevertheless, surely ecclesiastical politics and the problems of the relationship of the Welsh church to England and Rome were discussed by him and Baldwin during their seven weeks together.

Hereford cathedral boasts, in a new building opened in 1996 by Queen Elizabeth II, a chained library. This is reminiscent of a scriptorium which would have existed in the cathedral precincts in Gerald's day, in which the monks would have meticulously copied the religious and other

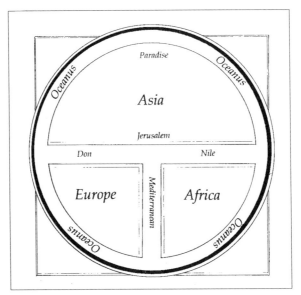

'T O' map

manuscripts handed down to them. It is also a fine reminder of the substantial library, which was at the disposal for study by the monks of the twelfth century. Many treasures that were owned by the cathedral are in the library, such as the eighth-century Hereford Gospels, and a wealth of magnificent illuminated works would have been equally accessible to Gerald.

Another treasure of the cathedral is the Mappa Mundi, but this is attributed to the late 1280s and would not have been available in Gerald's time. It is an important document of the Middle Ages and shows the concept of the centrality of Jerusalem in the minds of Christianity, especially during the times of the Crusades. These maps are known as 'T O' maps, the outside of the map being a circle (the 'O') and the world being split into three parts like a 'T', with the east being above the 'T'. The Mappa Mundi was in this form. It is said to have been compiled by Richard of Holdingham:

> Circular in form, with the east at the top, it shows representations of Paradise, Last Judgement, Pillars of Hercules and numerous biblical and other legends. Jerusalem is in the centre. The British Isles are shown on the edge of the map, bent round to fit in the circle, Scotland being separated from England.
>
> (Tooley)

Gerald himself was a cartographer of some note. In about 1200 he drew, amongst other maps, a 'Map of Europe', which shows the variety of land and river routes from Ireland and England to Rome. It is in the collection of the National Library of Ireland, Dublin. It is fair to say that neither map would be of much assistance to a modern traveller as their purpose is religious and not secular.

Also in the cathedral is one of the best-preserved

Cantilupe shrine, Hereford

medieval shrines in England. It is the stone and marble tomb of St Thomas de Cantilupe who was the Bishop of Hereford (1275–1282) and Chancellor of England. He was canonised in 1320.

Next door to the cathedral is the Bishop's Palace. This must have been where Archbishop Baldwin and Gerald were wined and dined before and after their journey. It obviously has been much modernised over the years but there still are remains of the twelfth-century palace itself. On entering the Great Hall one enters a roomy and light space with a high ceiling which runs across the width of the palace. This is in the style of Robert Adam and of the late eighteenth century. The original Great Hall ran along the length of the building, as can be seen by the roofline above the present palace. This would have been constructed of wood, possibly on a stone base. Inside one of the present pillars to the Hall, when the decorated casement is opened, there is revealed a well-preserved oak pillar which was one of the original supporting beams of the old Hall. It has been established that the timber-felling date of the oak beams of the palace was 1179, and thus it would have been contemporary with Gerald's visit.

The Hall would have been constructed with a high central roof with arcades on either side. Two of the oak half-braces, which may have been part of the arcades in the hall, can be seen, preserved, in the Tudor gateway to the Palace. Rather more bizarrely, on a wall abutting the Bishop's Palace, a notice commemorates the spot as the birthplace of Nell Gwynn, one of the best-known mistresses of King Charles II. She is remembered as an orange-seller outside the King's Theatre in London, from which she moved to be a comic actress before her career burgeoned into the royal bedchamber, amongst others. It was a short life, as well as a lively one, spanning the years 1650 to 1687.

Of the rest of Gerald's Hereford, little remains. A castle used to stand on Castle Green, built before the Norman Conquest of 1066. It was reconstructed by William Fitzobern in about 1070. It was attacked shortly after by Eadric the Wild, an Anglo-Saxon who was fighting against the Norman occupation, with the assistance of the Welsh.

The castle was subsequently enlarged in the twelfth century, so a structure certainly existed in 1188, but only the Castle Pool, a remnant of the moat, survives. St Peter's church was founded in the eleventh century by Walter de Lacy of Weobley but, sadly for him, in 1085 he fell to his death from the top of the building during its construction. Even though there were extensive renovations carried out in the eighteenth and nineteenth centuries parts of the old medieval church still are visible. The nave, built about 1300 on the foundations of the original church, is as wide as that of Hereford cathedral itself. St Peter's is alleged to have its own ghost, a cowled monk, which can walk through the solid doors of the church. It is thought to be the ghost of a medieval monk who was killed, but how, when and by whom remains a mystery.

So from the large City of Hereford, with all its treasures, Gerald set out on Friday 4 March 1188 along the Roman road toward Wales, following the banks of the Wye, probably with considerable trepidation about the future weeks. The countryside would have been very different from the beautiful and manicured fields we know today, but must nevertheless have been a rich and pleasant farming area with the spring growth and greenery emerging. It would vary depending on the area they passed through. It is probable that the fields covered between seven hundred acres and upwards and, rather than being surrounded by hedges and walls, were cultivated in long strips called furlongs, each about an acre in size. Two of every three furlongs would have been planted with a corn of some sort and the third left fallow and grazed by cattle, sheep, goats or sheep. In the higher areas used for sheep there would have been some enclosures for use in winter, but otherwise the country was largely grassland. Woodland areas were about the same as nowadays but would have been managed carefully. Every part of the woodland was used by those on the land as it was a basic right to collect fallen timber for fuel or any relevant purpose. But the variety of trees was different from today: there were far fewer conifers, and few evergreens except for holly, but, of course, the oak trees would have been very evident.

The road leads directly out west from Hereford and

passes through Bishopstone. Perhaps the name of the village is a reference to the passing of Archbishop Baldwin, as its name in the 1066 Domesday Book was Malveshill, but this is possibly just a romantic conjecture on my part. There is a small church at Bishopstone dedicated to St Lawrence, which was built in about 1125, and part of the Norman nave still is visible. The south transept is possibly of Roman origin as the remains of a Roman villa were found when the old rectory was built in 1812, but the foundations of the church are certainly Norman. It has a reredos which dates from about 1580 and shows a fine example of Elizabethan carving, although it has been restored subsequently. Passing through Bishopstone, the road soon swings north, with the Brecon Beacons away to the left, through the pretty timbered black-and-white village of Eardisley to Kington. It is possible that Gerald turned north earlier, but it would nice to think that he made a short detour through Weobley, a village also dating from the Doomsday Book of 1086, which was in the lordship of Walter de Lacy. But this is unlikely: his itinerary was not one of a tourist, but of a man with a mission. However, for modern travellers a visit to Weobley is worthwhile, particularly if time allows them to follow the history trail, where they will find remnants of buildings stretching back into the thirteenth century and before.

In 1188 Kington was a well-established town. Its existence was recorded both in the Domesday Book and also in the Pipe Rolls of 1187. As seems to occur in most of the towns through which Gerald passed there was a castle in close proximity to the church. The church is dedicated to Our Lady, St Mary the Virgin. It is thought that the Normans built the castles and churches close together as they regarded both edifices as part of the fortification of the towns. They were also specifically designed as a visible record of the power of the Normans and of their conquest and subjugation of the region. It also reinforced the very close connection between church and state. Kington castle was founded in about 1100 but abandoned in around 1173, when a rebellion by Roger de Port against King Henry II was quickly quashed. The Lordship passed to William de Broase, whose body is buried in Hereford cathedral. He was a dominant lord in the area, of whom we shall hear more. It is reasonable to state that, even if it had been in a run-down condition, the church would have still been standing when Gerald passed by. The church would have acted as an early reminder to Gerald, if he needed it, that de Port's rebellion was a mere fifteen years earlier, and that he still lived in uncertain times. It would therefore have been essential for him to have a large armed retinue both for security reasons as well as for status, even though the party were always under the protection of the various princes of Wales throughout their progression.

The church contains some relics which date back to Norman times, for example a Norman font, various stonemasons' marks and part of the tower, but many later additions are also worth seeing. For example, there is an

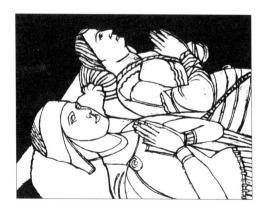

Tomb of Thomas Vaughan and Ellen the Terrible, Kington

alabaster tomb covering the body of Thomas Vaughan who died at the battle of Banbury in 1469. He was a supporter of the Yorkist cause. It is said that his ghost haunted the local lanes until twelve persons armed with twelve candles lured it into a silver snuffbox and cast it into Hergest pool nearby. Lewis Glyn Cothi, a famous Welsh bard, sang of Vaughan's deeds in an obituary to him. However, Vaughan's wife, Ellen Gethin, who is buried with him, was obviously not so regaled. She was known as Ellen the Terrible. She must have been as formidable as her name. Her reputation does not appear in her effigy as the face would seem to be of a fairly sweet-tempered lady, but perhaps this is the result of later renovations. At one time, dressed as a man, she attended an archery contest which was also attended by a relative who had killed her brother. Ellen, when her time for competing arrived, shot her arrow through the heart of her brother's assassin, killing him and escaping in the resulting confusion. Whether she earned the sobriquet of 'terrible' before or after this event is not known but she was clearly not a lady to be taken lightly!

Outside the church is a medieval preaching cross. There are several examples of preaching crosses in the open air throughout Wales, some of which date back to pre-Norman and even Saxon times. It was at such crosses that many sermons were delivered by Archbishop Baldwin and Gerald and it may be that they said a few words at the cross at Kington as they passed on their way. One is reminded by these crosses that, unlike today where services are held inside a church, in Gerald's time services were mainly in the open with marriages usually held on the church steps. The churches often were built like barns and were mainly used as shelters for pilgrims and locals including, one assumes, for services when the weather was inclement.

Gerald's party then pressed on up a valley with Hergest

Ridge to their left to reach New Radnor, where Archbishop Baldwin delivered a public sermon on the taking of vows to serve the cross in the Crusades. This was translated into Welsh by an interpreter. Gerald, eager to show his metal and to respond favourably to the Archbishop, was the first to volunteer and 'threw myself at the holy man's feet and devoutly took the sign of the cross'. This was possibly a piece of contrived theatre, with Gerald waiting for the first 'recruitment' meeting to take the cross publicly, so to encourage others to come forward and make sure the mission started off with a success. A form of early marketing!

The first day of their journey must have been a very busy one as New Radnor is some twenty-five miles from Hereford, which would have been a good day's ride for those on horses and very strenuous for the rest. Evidently the party stayed the night in the town as they celebrated mass in the early morning of the following day. They may have stayed at New Radnor castle, of which an impressive motte still remains and dominates the village. When one enters the village from the main road there is a large memorial to those who died in the wars and it is romantic to feel that this could have been the place where the sermons were delivered. Sadly that is unlikely, as this spot is some distance from both the church and the castle, and it was probably near the latter that Baldwin spoke, especially as there were many notabilities present, not least Rhys ap Gruffudd, prince of Deheubarth, under whose protection they were.

After mass Gerald states that they journeyed on to Cruker castle, some two miles from Radnor.

Hoare believes that Gerald back-tracked from New Radnor to Old Radnor, and that Cruker castle was next door to the church at Old Radnor. Thorpe agrees with this contention. Gerald would certainly have passed Old Radnor on the hill to his left on his way to New Radnor, and may possibly have visited it. But to retrace his steps seems strange and a waste of effort, certainly on the first day of the journey, unless, of course, the hospitality at Old Radnor was of a very high standard! It is much more probable that they would have carried on to the west of New Radnor, after mass, to Crug Eryr castle, which is now shown in the Ordnance Survey map as 'Cruker Castle'. There are remains in Old Radnor of a possible castle next to the church of St Stephen. It is a deeply-ditched site, but some historians now believe it to have been a building connected to the church, maybe for defence or as a rectory, but not a full-blown castle.

The church itself is worth a moment's pause to the modern visitor. It is built high above the valley at some 840 feet above sea level. Although much of the church has been rebuilt it has a very interesting carved medieval screen, reputed to be one of the finest in Wales, and there are remains of medieval floor tiles, a medieval book chain and a fine organ case and, amongst other artefacts, a pre-Norman font. The church also sports a fine timbered ceiling.

Assuming that Gerald did not turn back to Old Radnor but carried on westwards to the castle I believe to be Cruker he would have met with a motte-and-bailey castle built on a hill, from which the view across to the Black Mountains and the Brecon Beacons is superb on a clear day. On a wet windy March day the castle, being exposed on the top of a hill, might well have been fairly breezy! Gerald does not mention the clemency or otherwise of the weather, but at Cruker the Archbishop signed with the cross a 'robust and courageous young man' by the name of Hector, and also Maelgwn ap Cadwallon, prince of Maelienydd. They all spent two nights at the castle.

It is difficult through the fog of history to imagine the

Motte-and-bailey castle

hospitality and sleeping conditions that the party must have met on the way. Sometimes Gerald refers to being accommodated most comfortably, but it is interesting to hear his thoughts on the hospitality of the Welsh, as this gives a backdrop to their travels. He tells us that the homes of Welsh people were open to all. When travellers arrived they handed over their weapons and were given water to wash their feet. By so doing they became guests. They were entertained everywhere by the harp and other instruments:

> In the evening, when no more guests are expected, the meal is prepared according to the number and dignity of the persons assembled, and according to the wealth of the family which entertains; the kitchen does not supply many dishes, nor high seasoned incitements to eating; the house is not adorned with tables, cloths or napkins; they study nature more than splendour; for which reason they place all the dishes together upon mats, with large platters or trenchers full of sweet

herbs; they also make use of a thin and broad cake of bread, baked every day . . . and they sometimes add chopped meat with broth . . . While the family is engaged on waiting on the guests, the host and hostess stand up, paying unremitting attention to everything, and take no food till all the company are satisfied; that in case of any deficiency, it may fall upon them.

Thus life was fairly basic; by inference the hospitality of a Norman or royal household would have been much more lavish, with tablecloths, napkins and proper tables with tasty titbits and choice. Possibly the Normans' method of sleeping accommodation may have been similar to his description of the Welsh way: one would sleep in a bed stuffed with rushes on the floor and heated by an open fire, keeping one's clothes on for additional heat. A truckle bed would be a luxury, but nevertheless the mattress would still be one filled with reeds or hay. Even the most luxurious situation would have been pretty basic.

However, the fare of the monks would probably have been nearer to the basic Welsh hospitality – although their hospitality would have reflected the reputation and rank of both the hosts and their visitors.

Julie Kerr comments that there could be significant variations in religious hospitality. Sampson, Abbot of Bury St Edmunds in 1182, wanted to provide fitting hospitality as he did not want to get a reputation for meanness. On the other hand Robert of Meulan was regarded as stingy as he provided only one course in order to prevent indigestion! One imagines that Welsh hospitality to Gerald and his party was fairly generous, bearing in mind the nature of the travellers and that they were, in the main, being entertained by the abbots, bishops and princes of Wales. However, there would have been one difference between the secular and the religious houses: in the former there would have been music and entertainment, whereas in the latter there would have been readings from the Bible in an altogether more sober mode!

One of the enjoyments of reading Gerald's account of his journey is that he wanders off, from time to time, into various stories or myths about the region he is passing through. He relates several at this point in his book. These diversions are one of the charms of his writings and many are worth repeating, albeit not verbatim. Other later myths and stories are recounted which, had he been aware of them, I am sure he would have included in his account. One imagines him telling these glimpses of his time to entertain Baldwin and anyone else who was prepared to listen, possibly around an open fire at the end of a long day's journey, following the traditions of the travelling storytellers and troubadours. However, a quote from John of Salisbury in 1159 is very apposite both to Gerald's stories and those others added: 'I do not affirm that everything written here is true, but whether it be true or false, it will be useful to the reader ... Nonsense is combined here with serious things and lies with truth, so that everything leads to the higher virtue of supreme truth'. All history needs to be taken with a pinch of salt and the judgment of truth should be left to the reader!

The first of such stories concerns the castellan of Radnor castle. He sheltered the night with his dogs in the church of Saint Afan in a village nearby New Radnor called Llanafan. His choice of shelter was not a good move, for in the morning not only had his dogs gone mad but he had lost his sight. He was, needless to say, fairly fed up with living as a blind man so he decided to be led to Jerusalem and to join battle with the Crusaders. This he did, and was guided by his men to where the battle was fiercest, where he was struck down and killed by a sword. In Gerald's words he 'so ended his life with honour' in a true chivalric fashion. Gerald's moral is clear: namely, you should not stay with your hounds in a church or hallowed ground as the consequences can be fairly dire. Nevertheless, Llanafan is a fairly remote village so one can understand the castellan's dilemma of wishing to stay the night under shelter; his punishment seems harsh and not commensurate with his 'crime'!

Next to Llanafan church there is an old yew tree reputed to be over two thousand years old. Often old churches were built on sites where old pagan rites and worship had been carried out for centuries before Christianity. In addition, Andrew Morton tells us that the connection between the yew and churches in Wales developed further with the advent of the Celtic religion from Ireland, when many yews were planted. The sacredness of the tree was connected with individual Celtic saints who either lived beside an existing tree or planted a tree in the church of their foundation. Thus the combination of yew trees and a church confirms the old age of a church's foundation.

The village itself is small but there is an old public house across from the church which dates back some 550 years and sports a sign, updated each year, that it has been 'voted best pub in Llanafan for the 550th year running' or whatever the latest year is. Sadly, it was not around when the castellan was passing through, or his story would have had a much happier ending.

Hunting was obviously a dangerous pastime. Gerald tells us that in nearby Gwrthrynion a doe was killed by the attendant to Einion, son-in-law to the Lord Rhys, with whom they were travelling. The doe had large horns and was much larger than normal. Because of the size of the head and horns it was sent to King Henry II for his pleasure. Sadly the attendant who had killed the doe immediately fell ill, lost the sight of his right eye, simultaneously suffering a stroke, and remained feeble-minded and impotent for the rest of his life – presumably as he had not had the proper permission to kill the stag.

Gerald comments on the efficacy of local cures and miracles, giving the example of the miraculous staff, alleged to have belonged to Saint Curig, which was stored in a nearby church. The miracles surrounding the staff, which was encased in gold and silver, were highly commercial as, for a penny, tumours or glandular swellings were cured by the staff's application to the relevant part of the body. Sadly one supplicant paid only half price and had only half a cure, but when he paid up the full sum he was fully cured. Another tried to pay on credit but when the due date came and he did not pay his dues the tumour returned. Luckily, after a payment of the much-increased price of three pence, all came well!

In Llywel, a small village about a mile from Trecastle on the Llandovery road, the church, Gerald tells us, 'was burned down by the enemy and everything was destroyed, except one small box, in which the consecrated host had been deposited'. Who 'the enemy' were is not recorded; it was possibly a local raid, but at least the holy box was saved.

In Glascwm, through which the party probably passed on its way to Hay-on-Wye, there was said to be a miraculous handbell, a *bangu*, which had allegedly belonged to St David. A woman stole it to use its miraculous powers to free her husband, who was chained up in a nearby castle. The keepers of the castle refused to free her husband and stole the bell from her. Retribution inevitably followed and the whole town was burnt down – except for the wall upon which the *bangu* was hanging. One assumes the poor husband perished, but I suppose as his wife had stolen the bell this was only to be expected.

Finally he relates two miraculous happenings surrounding the death of both Henry I and Henry II. On the death of Henry I in 1135 it was reported that two large pools, one artificial and one natural, broke their banks. Of the artificial pool all was lost, but the natural pool, possibly a lake mentioned by Leland, in Lower Elvel or Elvelia, was re-established some two miles away with all its wild life and fish intact. After the death of Henry II in 1189 at Chinon, it was said that in a pool in Normandy there was a huge battle of fish, all of which died, but this event presaged the death of one particular man, presumably the king. Such were some of the stories of twelfth-century Wales; indeed, many of the pools and lakes of Wales have myths and legends surrounding them.

Chapter 2
Hay-on-Wye and Brecknockshire

After their stay at Cruker the party, on Monday 7 March, rode down the valley along one of the many pathways running south, crossing the Wye at Hay-on-Wye. This was a much more direct route than the present road which passes through Hundred House and then drops down through several country lanes to Hay. Gerald does not comment on the precise route he used, but he might well have passed close to the church and settlement of Glascwm which was referred to in the previous chapter. It is thought, partially because of his reference to Glascwm, that he and Baldwin visited the church. Glascwm itself sits in a deep valley bowl. The little eleventh-century church is dedicated to St David, to which his miraculous handbell (*bangu*), having been stolen, was eventually returned. Strange as it may seem, the first object one sees on entering St David's is a large bell, but sadly there the coincidence ends, as it is an old bell from the bell tower and has no intrinsic miraculous powers.

But it does have its own history. It was founded in 1735. Apparently, five years earlier in 1730 the church wardens had reported that 'one of the bells is crakt.' It was brought down to its present resting place from the tower during the revelry of a wedding party by some of the guests who were a little out of hand. A similar story is told by Kilvert in 1870. He tells that:

> There used to be three good bells in Glascwm church brought by the enchanted bisons from Llan-ddewi Brefi. Just before the present Vicar came there was a tremendous wedding of a farmer's daughter. There was great enthusiasm and excitement and the bells

were required to ring very loud. One bell did not ring loud enough to satisfy the people so they took an axe up to the bell and beat the bell with an axe till they beat it all to pieces.

This would imply that a similar event had happened in the eighteenth century as well. Was this the same bell and story or was Glascwm an area where there were a series of riotous weddings? Whatever date the bell was brought down from the tower, the story of its descent rings true, even if the bell did not! Presumably because of the connection with St David's miraculous bell the *bangu* retained a religious significance and was used in the home of someone who has died. It was taken to the home of the deceased and remained there until the funeral service when it is taken to the church, together with the deceased, ringing in the forefront of the of the funeral procession. Hoare states that *bangus* were still in use in this way until 1800 at Caerleon, and they were rung just before the internment.

Glaswm was originally a settlement based on an old Celtic religious tradition and was the centre of monasticism. Indeed the name of such a Celtic group was a '*clas*' and with the Welsh name for valley being 'cwm', the derivation of the village name is clear. The '*clas*' monasteries were of particular interest. They were literally family-based, and their members did not follow the vows of celibacy as did other orders such as the Benedictines. The abbots were hereditary, unlike other monastic rules. Whilst the monks would have served the spiritual needs of the area round Glascwm, the settlement itself, being fairly isolated, provided the solitude for contemplation. It was built close to a small river, which would have served the daily needs of the monks as well as being on hand for baptisms – not least, for the community's own children. The '*clas*' system was broken up by the Normans and replaced by the parish system. Gerald did not approve of the '*clas*' system and in particular the hereditary succession within the '*clas*'.

On their way to Hay-on-Wye it is just conceivable that Gerald could have passed the church at Newchurch, outside of which runs Offa's Dyke, which was constructed during the reign of Offa, king of Mercia (757–96) in order to clarify the route of the boundary between Mercia and Powys.

Gerald may also have passed through Painscastle. As its name suggests, there are the remains of a castle originally built by Pain Fitz-John but destroyed in 1137. It was rebuilt and by the time of Gerald's journey was held by William de Broase. In 1195 William defeated the Welsh from the castle. Rhys ap Gruffudd beseiged the castle in 1196 but failed to take it. In 1198 Gwenwynwyn of Powys attached the castle, because he was incensed that his cousin Talhaiarn had been dragged through Brecon tied to a horse, and had then been beheaded.

Gerald's details of his actual journey are characteristically sparse but he comments that they crossed the Wye into Hay. A sermon was delivered at Hay castle, presumably by the Archbishop, after which a great number of men came running towards Baldwin to take the Cross, leaving their cloaks in the hands of their wives and friends who had tried to restrain their enthusiasm.

The castle mound still dominates the town. Hay-on-Wye now has the reputation as 'the town of books', with somewhere in excess of forty bookshops available to the browser, researcher and reader, and is renowned for its annual literary festival at the end of May each year when the small market town is flooded with thousands of visitors.

No doubt the modern Gerald would have his own bookshop, selling his various works and trying to reverse the trend in reading of his own time. He would have approved of learning from books. In the preface to his 'Journey' he writes that whereas 'literary fame, which used to be placed in the highest rank, is now, because of the depravity of the times, tending to ruin and degraded to the lowest, so that persons attached to the study are at present not imitated or venerated, but even detested'. This is, of course, with the exception of Gerald himself, whose love is that of letters. Through his writing he tells us that he hopes to attain his ambition. 'As this life is temporary and mutable, it is grateful to live in the memory of future ages and to be immortalised by fame'. This he has indeed achieved despite his innate modesty!

The present castle was built around 1200 by William de Braose II, a notorious Norman Marcher lord, and it is alleged that it was physically built in one night by his wife who carried the necessary stones for the entire edifice in her apron. His wife, known alternately as Matilda, Maud de St Valery, or Moll Walbee, was said to have been a witch and also a giant (yet another one!), and that she had the strength and the ability to hurl boulders more than a mile. Due to her enormous size and bravado she was said to be able to achieve miracles such as building the castle. Sadly she met a difficult end, together with her unfortunate son. When she became too troublesome for King John to handle, he had her and her son entombed alive at Corfe Castle with only a piece of raw bacon and one sheaf of wheat between them. After a somewhat unreasonable period of eleven days they were dug out from the dungeon, but they were long dead.

After spending the Monday night (7 March) at Hay Gerald's party journeyed on along the Wye valley to Llanddew, where they would have stayed either at the Bishop of Brecon's palace or, perhaps more likely, at Gerald's home, which was next door. Of the two buildings little remains, but Gerald was obviously fond and proud of his residence. This he had by dint of his holding the post of Archdeacon of Brecon from 1175 to 1203. He writes:

> In these temperate regions, I have obtained (according to the usual expression) a place of dignity, but of no great omen of future pomp or riches; and possessing a small residence near the castle of Brecheinoc, well adapted to literary pursuits, and to the contemplation of eternity, I envy not the riches of Croesus; happy and contented with that mediocrity, which I prize far beyond all the perishable and transitory things of this world.

Certainly the setting for the house or palace, be it what it was, is very peaceful, across from the village church. Some remains of the castellated building still remain, as does the remnant of an attractive arched doorway (possibly of a later

Gerald's gate, Llan-ddew

period), a wall and small garden. Gerald's spirit seems to be there; one can envisage him spending times of contemplation both in the garden and the little parish church of St David across the road, and also conversing with the Bishop from time to time.

Further up the lane from the remains of his house is Bishop Gower's Well. This is unusual as it is available to users on both sides of the wall surrounding the palace, enabling the commoners outside the palace to share the waters with those inside the gardens.

Llan-ddew church dates back to AD 500 when it is chronicled that Aled, daughter of Brychan, fled there for sanctuary. A lintel of the great door exists from the early eleventh century as does a piscina in the south transept. The rest of the church is later. The oldest part is the chancel. This is built, as indeed it is in many churches, slightly out of line with the line of the tower and nave slightly offset. This is a 'weeping chancel', said to represent the inclination of Christ's head on the cross. In each vestry are what are called squints or hagioscopes (lovely words), holes in the walls that allowed priests celebrating communion in the transepts to follow the same timing as the priest at the main altar. These are visible at several of the churches in Wales, as are 'weeping chancels'. Judging by the size of the church and the fact there were two palaces in Gerald's day, the village must have been a lively place, but it is now a gentle and tranquil town.

From Llan-ddew they moved on to Brecon. One week after the journey had started they probably returned to stay the night at Llan-ddew again. While at Llan-ddew Gerald, as Archdeacon of Brecon, presented Baldwin with his work, Topographia Hibernica (*Topography of Ireland*). 'He graciously received it, and either read or heard a part of it read every day during his journey; and on his return to

England completed the perusal of it'. Gerald may well have read it to Baldwin himself to make sure that due care and attention was given to his book!

Brecon was the chief town of the district at the time, sporting both a castle and a cathedral. It is built on the confluence of the rivers Honddu and Usk. The cathedral is on the site of a Benedictine Priory, founded in 1093, and was linked to the Benedictine house of Battle in Sussex. It was established by Bernard de Neufmarche who also built the castle nearby. The castle would have been very substantial when Gerald visited Brecon, being a highly strategic site, although most of the surviving structure dates to the middle of the thirteenth century.

The old Norman remains of the cathedral, which Gerald would have known, are sparse and only the font and stonework in the east end of the nave remain. The font is carved with grotesque masks, fantastic birds and beasts, all intertwined. The present church dates from two main phases of construction, one from 1200 and the other from the fourteenth century, and of course, thereafter. The Harvard Chapel, named after a local family, was built in the fourteenth century as a chantry chapel replacing two earlier ones. It is dedicated to the South Wales Borderers Regiment (later amalgamated into the Royal Regiment of Wales) which was much involved in the battles at Isandlhwana and Rourke's Drift in the Zulu wars of 1879 in South Africa. The chapel is home to a fourteenth-century tomb and boasts a squint looking up to the high altar. Parts of the monastic buildings still exist, as does a cresset stone which was an early medieval method of lighting that would have held some thirty candles. In the graveyard lie the tombs of a French officer who died at Brecon at the time of the Napoleonic wars, and that of one of the first British soldiers to be awarded a Victoria Cross. In the cathedral, amongst many other areas of interest, is a guild chapel for the Corvisors or Cordwainers, who were shoemakers and who controlled the trade in the area in medieval times.

Gerald, having reached Brecon, meanders off in his inimitable style to tell various contemporary local stories and anecdotes. He first relates how he was approached by a priest, Hugh, who had a vision telling him to challenge William de Broase, the Norman Marcher lord, to return certain properties to the church which William had claimed for himself. Gerald was not overly helpful to Hugh, as all he did was point out that the vision was from St Augustine and meant that as de Broase was not paying his church dues and tithes he would end up in trouble! Gerald tells us that de Broase was much condemned for his practices but he doesn't seem to have suffered unduly, being rich and powerful. Gerald was not a keen adherent of de Broase but obviously had to steer a careful course between his spiritual and temporal masters. He manifestly disliked both William and his wife Matilda, who we have already met, and says, somewhat ironically, 'both of whom, I hope, by their devotion obtained temporal happiness and grace, as well as the glory of eternity.'

He tells of a boy who attempted to steal some pigeons from a nest in the tower of Llan-faes church. The boy's hands stuck fast to a stone on which he was leaning, a punishment from St David, and it was only after three days and much prayer that he was released by the same divine intervention. Gerald says he actually met the boy in later life and that his finger marks were still visible in the stone. A woman in Bury St Edmunds had a somewhat similar 'sticky' time. She was wont to steal from the offertory, and her lips stuck fast to the altar until she spat out a silver coin which she had hidden in her mouth. Rather more excitingly, a parson's girlfriend sat on a saint's tomb in a church on

Humberside and her backside stuck to the tomb. Her clothes had to be cut off until she was naked when, after divine intervention, she was allowed to go home!

Misbehaviour and sticking to holy relics was clearly very much a way of life, as was demonstrated by a cellarer from Winchcombe in Gloucestershire. He had intercourse with a local woman within the confines of an abbey. The following day his hands stuck to a holy Psalter, but after repentance he was freed. Nothing is heard of the woman in question. The Psalter belonged to Quendrada, who was sister of St Kenelm whom she had murdered. Divine retribution came to Quendrada, when her eyes were torn from her head, falling plop on the book. The bloodstains could be seen even in Gerald's time. He comments on several relics, for example St Cynog's miraculous torque and St Patrick's horn, and the problems which befell those who misused them.

He tells us of many strange events which had happened in his lifetime. For example, a sow, which had been suckled by a dog, became a hunter of game, and a knight gave birth to a calf! He also mentions that when St Illtyd was living at Llanhamlach, a village close to Brecon, his mare was covered by a stag and the progeny had the front half of a horse and the haunches of a stag, enabling it to run at great speed. These strange animals were usually regarded as portents of a great calamity in the middle ages, but Gerald does not make mention of any arising from these occurrences. Certainly it would seem that in Gerald's time life was full of excitement and strange happenings which makes modern life seem quite tame in comparison.

Near Llanhamlach is a long barrow called Ty Illtud or Saint Illtud's house. The saint lived as a hermit, dying about 540, and according to Hoare his house was composed of three stones pitched in the ground supporting a fourth on top in the same form as an entrance to a barrow and similar to a cromlech. These were excavated in the nineteenth century, presumably before Hoare's visit, and apparently more than sixty inscribed crosses and symbols are visible on the stones, although these inscriptions are of a much later date than the erection of the chamber. It is open to conjecture as to whether Illtud actually made use of this Neolithic burial chamber as his hermit's retreat. In Llanhamlach churchyard are several old yew trees and in the church itself are the remains of the Moridic Stone. This is a Christian memorial stone dating from no later than the eleventh century and possibly two or three centuries earlier. It depicts a cross with the top missing, with a male figure to the left and, surprisingly, a larger female figure to the right, but this possibly may have been to emphasise the importance of the Virgin at that time. It bears the inscription *'Johannis ... Moridic surrexit'* meaning 'Johannis Moridic is risen'. In the porch of the church are several old gravestones.

Gerald did not pass through Llanhamlach on this journey but he tells many detailed and contemporary stories concerning local towns and their personages. One or two will be related here.

Bernard de Neufmarche married his wife Agnes and had children by her, including one Mahel. Mahel returned home one night to find his mother committing adultery and, not unnaturally, created an uproar. His mother was not too pleased and after a long and acrimonious life she managed to ruin both herself, her son and her family. Gerald concludes that women are nothing but trouble and indeed that 'women to gratify one inclination, will not scruple to perpetrate all sorts of wickedness'. He would not have been able to make such comments nowadays, and indeed, even at that time he attributed the concept to Tully!

Having castigated women he mentions that a man named Brachanus had some twenty-four daughters, all of whom followed a religious career, and states that many churches are named after them. One, St Eluned, had a church named after her, which was still standing in 1698 on the spot where she was martyred. Each August there used to be a festival at which many came to seek recovery from their illnesses. Also many young people came to dance and celebrate. After dancing they suddenly leapt into the air and then, as suddenly, collapsed as in a frenzy, wakening in due course to mime various actions, some guiding their cattle singing as they went, one imitating a tanner, another a cobbler with the women using a distaff, until they all went back into church. Once in the church they would wake as if from a trance. Whether this was alcoholically induced or a form of mass hysteria we are not told. As the region produces a lot of corn, according to Gerald, had the young people eaten or drunk from the crop product they could have suffered from a form of ergot poisoning from old and damp wheat, and this could have caused the 'madness' they incurred. Whatever the reason for the strange goings-on it would seem, from the way Gerald relates them, that he probably had witnessed the celebrations at first hand. Who can gainsay, but it all sounds great fun in the tradition of feasts and holidays when topsy-turveydom ruled, allowing the peasants to let off steam once a year and even reverse roles with their landlords, so ably described by Mikhail Bakhtin as a basic rite and activity of the middle ages.

Concerning the dancers and tumblers Hoare says 'From this account of Giraldus, we might almost suppose that our modern jumpers (so numerous throughout Wales) are the descendants of these votaries of Saint Aled'. Hoare refers here to those affected by the religious revival of Llangeitho in 1762, who had a habit of jumping for joy during services, and were therefore known as 'jumpers'.

Gerald refers to a nearby lake now called Llan-gors (*Llyn*

Statue of Gerald of Wales,
Llandaff cathedral, Cardiff

Statue of Gerald of Wales,
St David's cathedral

Hereford cathedral: the start and finish of the journey

Preaching cross, Kington

The old bell at Glascwm

Brecon cathedral,
where Gerald was Archdeacon

Llanthony: St David's chapel

Partrishow: the preaching cross and
tabernacle

Usk castle: central court, with geese

The rood loft and screen at Partrishow

The millennium tapestry, Abergavenny

The Roman amphitheatre, Caerleon

*Llandaff: Cathedral Green
and preaching cross*

*Sir Jacob Epstein's statue
'Christ in majesty', Llandaff*

Abbey chancel, Neath

Pembrey: the white church tower

The entrance to Gerald's home, Manorbier

Manorbier: view of the castle and beyond

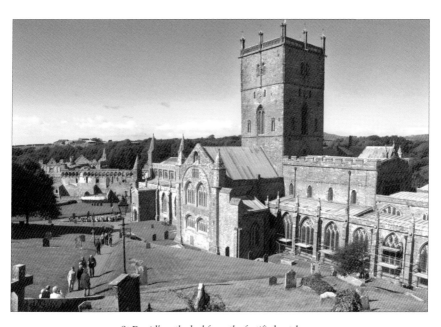

St David's cathedral from the fortified gatehouse

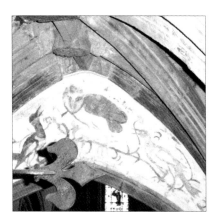

*St David's cathedral: an owl
taunted by two magpies*

*The tomb of the Lord Rhys
in St David's cathedral*

St Non's well, near St David's

St David's: Bishop Gower's Palace

The Norman gateway at Strata Florida

*The tombs of the Princes of Wales,
Strata Florida*

Llanbadarn: Celtic stone cross

The Cadfan stone, Tywyn

Harlech castle with the Snowdon range in the distance

Cricieth castle

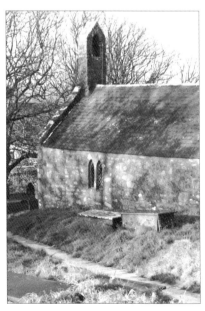

Pistyll: the pilgrimage chapel of St Beuno

Clynnog Fawr: St Beuno's church

The Eagle Tower, Caernarfon Castle

Anglesey, Priestholm or Puffin island

Beaumaris castle on Anglesey

The Church of St Mary and All Saints, Conwy

Conwy castle

Nant Peris: the pass between the Glyder and Snowdon mountain ranges

Looking across to Snowdon from Llynnau Mymbyr

The new castle, Rhuddlan

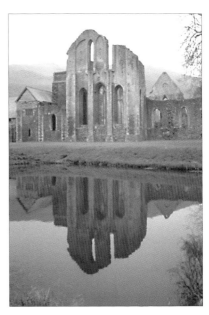

Glyn y Groes Abbey

St Winefride's well

Inside the nave of Chester cathedral

Chester cathedral

Shrewsbury abbey and refectory pulpit

Stokesay castle, a fortified merchant's dwelling

Ludlow castle: St Mary Magdalene church   *St Lawrence church, Ludlow*

Leominster: the priory and parochial church

Syfaddan), telling the myth that if the true ruler of the land arrived at the lake and ordered the birds to sing they would do just that. Gruffudd ap Rhys ap Tewdr came to the lake and, after praying to God, the birds duly obliged, much to his gratification. The lake was, and may still be, well stocked with fish, but it also was held to have miraculous properties. For example from time to time it would turn bright green or scarlet. The Reverend Evans recalls that:

> After great rains Lleveny pours down from the mountains in such a rage as to bring much soil with it, assumes a red colour and is distinguished flowing through the lake. It is said that a little before the invasion of the country by the Normans and English, 1030, the waters of the Lleveny, coloured a green colour, which quickly changed into blood red; and a similar phenomenon took place before the sanguinary war of the sons of Jestin.

Myths have a habit of being based to some extent on fact. Gerald recalls that those who live near Llan-gors observed that the lake was covered with gardens, orchards and buildings. If one visits nowadays you can see the lake with several artificial islands. These are made by infilling a staked artificial island. In medieval times they were probably constructed so that the inhabitants could better defend themselves from animal and human attack. It is recorded that over 1000 years ago a stockaded artificial island (a 'crannock') was built a little way out into the lake and that remains of massive log canoes have been found dating back to about 800. Maybe these are also reminiscent of the floating islands we will meet in Snowdonia. There is also a myth that there was once a wicked city submerged in the lake. In a 1695 document at the British Library (Harleian

MS. No. 7017) it is recorded that:

> In the greate Poole call'd Llyn Savathan once stood a
> faire citie which was swallowed up in an Earthquake
> and resigned her stone walles into this deep and
> broad water, being stored most richly with fish in such
> abundance as is incredible ... and the fishermen of this
> place have often times taken up goodes of several
> sortes from the very harte of the Poole but whether
> these might be goodes that were cast away in crossing
> the water is unknowne but we have never heard of any
> such mischance in oure time.

Another legend is told about this city. Local stories suggest
that the land beneath the lake once belonged to a cruel and
greedy princess. She had a lover who was poor. Nevertheless
she agreed to marry him – but only if he brought her great
riches. So the lover set out to make his fortune. In the event
he murdered and robbed a wealthy merchant, taking all his
fortune, which he presented to his princess. However, the
merchant's ghost returned to warn the happy couple that
their crime would be avenged. Strangely, his vengeance
would not fall on them but on the ninth generation of their
family, which seems somewhat unfair to their eventual
relatives. One night, years later, a great flood burst from the
hills drowning the surrounding land and its inhabitants –
and this is the city which can be seen under the water.

Chapter 3
Ewias and Llanthony

Gerald strays from his actual journey to describe what may well have been his favourite abbey, that of the Augustinian canons (the Black Canons) at Llanthony. Surprisingly, despite Llanthony being one of his preferred places, Gerald and Baldwin did not visit the abbey on their journey. But there was a long way to go, and a stay of self-indulgence was not on the agenda particularly so early in the tour. Nevertheless, it is well worth the modern visitor deviating up the valley of the Honddu to see the ruins, which are in a most peaceful and glorious setting in the fold of the river valley. So, unlike Gerald, we will deviate both physically and in spirit and visit Llanthony.

Gerald describes the site of Llanthony as being in a deep valley of the Ewias, shut in on all sides by a ring of high mountains. The valley is, according to Hoare's translation, 'about an arrow shot broad'; Thorpe translates it as 'three arrow shots', which is probably more realistic. Whichever is correct, this gives one some feeling of how far the longbow could fire in 1198. It has been recently estimated that a Welsh longbow archer could easily shoot an arrow up to 200 metres and so the valley was some 600 to 750 metres wide.

The church Gerald knew was the abbey church of St John the Baptist, which was built around 1180. He also knew the small church that is now just outside the abbey grounds. It had been built, according to him, on the spot where there had previously been a small chapel dedicated to St David. The title of Llanthony, Gerald tells us, was derived from the word 'llan' which means a religious place, and Honddu, the name of the river in the valley. Gerald also tells us that derivation could come from the local name at that time, Llan-ddewi Nant Honddu, meaning the church of David on the Honddu. St David had built a cell there during the sixth century, which had fallen into ruin until William de Lacy, who was hunting in the vicinity, came across the remains of the hermitage and was so overcome by the wish to mend his evil ways that he decided to spend his remaining life to rebuilding the chapel and to contemplation.

There is a fascinating legend concerning William de Lacy. It is alleged that having founded the chapel of Llanthony he never, for the rest of his life, removed his armour. Whether this was as a penance or because of the onset of rust and corrosion from the dank atmosphere in the valley or other reasons is not recorded. Nevertheless, it must have been a very uncomfortable experience. However, whether the legend is true or not, by 1108 he and a priest Ernisius had built the first priory church of Llanthony.

The little church is plain in construction and almost unchanged from the eleventh-century church which Gerald would have visited. Its thick walls and small windows remind us that part of its purpose was as a place of refuge. The church is oriented to the date of 1 March, celebrated as St David's day, as the altar is sited in such a way so that rays from the rising sun will hit it on that morning. When the main abbey was in its heyday the chapel became an infirmary, meeting both the needs of the monks and surrounding area. It has now reverted to its original function as a place of constant worship.

Gerald relates that the downfall of Llanthony Priory was due to mismanagement. Llanthony was:

> a spot truly fitted for contemplation, a happy and delightful spot, fully competent, from its first establishment, to supply all its own wants, had not the extravagance of English luxury, the pride of

sumptuous table, the increasing growth of intemperance and ingratitude, added to the negligence of its patrons and prelates, reduced it from freedom to servility; and if the step-daughter, no less enviously than odiously, had not supplanted her mother.

The sister house is in Gloucester, and most of the books in the Library together with all its wealth were transferred there under the sixth Prior, Roger of Norwich (1174?–c.1189). There was no love lost between Gerald and the latter management! He discusses the nature and criticisms of the various religious orders and admits that the Augustinians were probably preferable to the others, but in his view the lust for possessions in everyone leads to greed and corruption. He tells the story that a member of the clergy by name Fulk, who is possibly Fulk of Neuilly who preached the cross to great effect in France, was in discussion with King Richard I (The Lionheart) and set him a conundrum:

'You have three daughters namely Pride, Luxury and Avarice, and as long as they shall remain with you, you can never expect to be in favour with God.' To which the King, after a short pause, replied: 'I have already given away those daughters in marriage. Pride to the Templars, Luxury to the Black Monks [the Benedictines] and Avarice to the White [the Cistercians].'

A slightly different version is given by Holinshed, who ascribes lechery to the prelates of the church. Gerald's commentary is an interesting comment on the church of his time and how, despite the good and holy beginnings of the various Orders, they and the church were changing for the worse under the evil effects of wealth, abuse of power, and the greed and covetousness which comes from too much good living.

Returning to the ruins of Llanthony, a good place to start out to see the remains of the site is from the bar. This is the splendidly vaulted undercroft of the canon's and possibly the prior's residence which dates from the late 1100s. It is good to think that perhaps Gerald once visited the establishment and tasted its good victuals, as can the present-day traveller. The abbey church he would have known, and while the present nave was possibly built a little later than his time the north and south transepts, the canon's quire and the Presbytery were contemporary, as were the two chapels leading off from the transept and the quire. The organisation of the priory buildings is in a format that seems to apply to all abbeys and priories and certainly sets a pattern we will see throughout Wales, with some variations in size and wealth, so it is a convenient moment to comment on the layout of Llanthony.

The dominant feature is the church itself. This is laid out as a cruciform with the nave leading up to the canon's quire. The quire would have been separated from the nave by a screen to enable the monks to worship away from the gaze of the laity. The quire itself is flanked by the north and south transepts and leads into the presbytery and high altar that again is flanked by two chapels. To the south side of the church is the large cloister, enclosed round the ambulatory but open in the centre to the elements. The cloister, in its turn, is surrounded by the administrative and living quarters of the prior and the monks, with a refectory, dormitories, chapter house and buildings for hospitality to visitors and travellers. Outside would have been the farm and fishponds and, as it was vital to life, a copious supply of water, in this

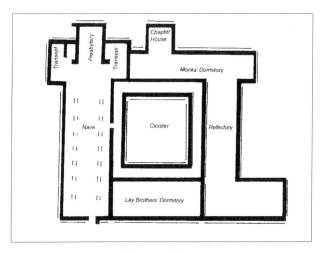

Monastery layout

case the Honddu. The whole would have been dominated by the towers to the west end of the church and the central tower, and in most cases would have been protected by a wall encircling the entire site with a formidable gatehouse to safeguard the incumbents from unacceptable visitors.

It is surprising that Gerald and Baldwin did not stay at the Priory as they passed nearby. Maybe this was due to the problems Gerald had referred to, as perhaps the transfer of Llanthony's wealth to its sister Priory at Gloucester had affected it to such an extent that it was no longer a sufficiently hospitable place to stay. Perhaps, and more likely, he did not see the isolated Llanthony as a place where he could recruit a great number to take the cross and it was thus not worthy of a deviation. Whatever the reason we, like Gerald, will return to the journey, moving off from his house in Llan-ddew.

Chapter 4
Coed Grwyne and Abergavenny

Gerald is very specific in the route the party took from Llan-ddew on Thursday 10 March, telling us that they followed the path down the pass of Coed Grwyne along a narrow track surrounded by trees, passing Llanthony over on the left. When consulting a modern map this seems both a longer and more difficult way to travel, although the old main road from Talgarth and mid Wales to Abergavenny apparently followed this route. The choice of route would not have been because of the stunning scenery of the area; I doubt that would have been uppermost in Gerald's mind.

Hoare comments in more detail on the route, which was still in use in 1806, and may well have followed it himself. He states:

> It appears then, that from Llan-ddew he took the road to Talgarth, from whence, climbing up a steep ascent, now called Rhys Constable, or the Constable's ascent he crossed the black mountains of Llanelli to the source of the Gronwy-fawr river, which rises in that eminence, and pursues its rapid course into the vale of the Usk. From thence a rugged and uneven track descends suddenly into a narrow glen, formed by the torrent of the Gronwy, between steep impending mountains black and barren for the first four or five miles but afterward wooded to the very margin of the stream. This road at length emerging from the deep recess of Coed Groen or Cwm Gronwy, crosses the river at a place called Port Escot, or the Bishop's bridge, probably so called from the very circumstance of its having now been passed by the Archbishop and

his suite, and is continued through the forest of Moel till it joins the Hereford road, about two miles from Abergavenny.

But why did they take such a roundabout route, particularly as they did not visit Llanthony? Hoare's explanation is that they wished to explore the interior of the land in order to encourage the local population to support the cross. This does not seem immediately evident as Gerald only records that they came to Abergavenny and mentions nothing else. However, local tradition claims that Gerald preached the cross from the churchyard cross at Partrishow (*Patrisio*). If it was on the main road of the time, Partrishow may well have been a much more populous place than its present isolation implies.

Nowadays the church at Partrishow is found up many winding lanes and is an absolute gem of a church to visit. Due to Partrishow's isolation it was largely spared the

Preaching cross, Partrishow

Tracery, Partishow

vandalism and iconoclasm of the reformist movement and thus has many features dating from the middle ages. Outside the church are found the remains of the cross from which Gerald or Baldwin may have preached. The preaching cross still stands despite the ordering of the destruction of all such crosses in 1547. The cross has a modernised tabernacle top with a statue to St Issui, who had a cell and well nearby, the Virgin, the Crucifixion and, last but not least, Archbishop Baldwin himself. Inside the church is a rare fifteenth-century rood loft and screen, delicately carved, which shows on one beam a dragon consuming a vine. The screen, which is carved from Irish oak, was never painted and is thus in its original state. It has a walkway above.

The chapel contains a stone altar with six consecration crosses. This is unusual: such altars normally have only five crosses incised. The records show that about 1150 the church of Merthyr Issui was consecrated. The large font was constructed some 100 years before Gerald's visit and would have been there in 1188. However, the interior would have been different, not least in its decorations. Painted on the west wall of the Nave is a coloured skeleton, holding a scythe, an hourglass and a spade, depicting 'Time'.

King James I ordered that all such paintings be covered up as, in his view, they were remnants of Roman Catholicism. Instead the walls should be whitewashed and be adorned only with suitable scriptural texts. However, the painting of 'Time' seems to have escaped such a stricture, probably due to the remoteness of the church. Partrishow has painted texts in abundance, but still some pre-Reformation painting can be discerned around the texts in addition to 'Time'. There is also a rare garter surrounding a painting of the Royal Arms on the north nave. The chancel is Elizabethan but much of the church can be traced further back in time and a visit to the church of Merthyr Issui at Partrishow leaves an unforgettable memory.

It is a reasonable assumption that Gerald and Baldwin passed through Partrishow and that the local tradition of their having preached there is very believable. After such a brief stop the party continued on to Abergavenny, where they probably stayed at the castle; a sermon was delivered there, encouraging many to take the cross.

Near Abergavenny, two buildings are worthy of note for the present traveller. The first is the bizarre church at Cwmyoy which was constructed, again, by the Normans. It is fascinating as its tower, walls, floor and indeed virtually every plane are at odd angles. It is a distinctly 'wobbly' church. This is due to various landslides, but rather than building afresh the then villagers used buttresses and all methods they could find to support the building. Jenkins mentions a local joke that the church is only for those 'so inclined'.

The other building, Tretower, is further back off the A40 towards Brecon, and is passed to the left by the modern

Stone carving, Cwmyoy

traveller. The tower can be clearly seen just off the main road and is of itself of interest but attached to it, according to Jenkins, is the most extensive medieval house in Wales, showing the way such houses were developed from the Norman time through the Middle Ages until its rebuilding in the fifteenth and sixteenth centuries. There is a fine medieval hall to add to the Norman motte-and-bailey. The tower and court are now open to the public again after refurbishment.

On to Abergavenny. Abergavenny castle was the site of the Archbishop's sermon. The castle stands high above the confluence of the rivers Gafenni and Usk. Gerald refers to the infamy in the time of our friend William de Broase as 'blood thirsty outrages'. He does not ascribe them specifically to de Broase but says that others can tell the tale rather than him. As de Broase was still a very powerful Baron one assumes that Gerald did not want to cause offence unnecessarily! The tale is that on Christmas Day William de

Broase murdered a long standing rival to him, Seisyllt ap Dyfnwal, and all his men in the great hall of the castle.

The details are related by Holinshed. He tells us that William, having gathered Seisyllt and great number of Welshmen into the castle, under the pretext of improving communication, proposed that an ordinance should be sworn by all of them together under oath that no traveller amongst them should bear any bow or other arms. They refused, not unnaturally, to take such an oath, as it was far from reasonable, especially as it was being imposed on them, under duress, by their greatest enemy.

William, in retaliation for their obduracy, condemned them all to death and the Great Hall became a feast of murder rather than a meal of peace. In retaliation the castle was burnt by Hywel ap Iorweth in 1182. Gerald relates that the incumbents were encouraged by the besiegers to stay up all night as they expected an attack which never came. However, in the morning they took off their armour to relax, supposing the threat to have gone away, and were attacked and overthrown.

This sacking of the castle happened a mere six years before Gerald's visit and it is thus surprising that there was anywhere to stay or preach. The castle had been rebuilt swiftly, bearing in mind its strategic location, probably as a timber building, but there is also a slight possibility that the master tower at Abergavenny was constructed in stone. The castle was again destroyed in 1233 by the Welsh Princes so that the present imposing ruins are from the thirteenth and fourteenth century and later, and it boasts an even later Victorian keep in which there is now a small museum. What remains is still impressive and in Leland's time he stated that the walls were 'likely not to fall', but the ravages of the Civil War and time have taken their toll.

Abergavenny was a centre of an interesting past when

Gerald was there and then, as now, St Mary's Priory was in existence, having been founded by Hamelin de Ballon in 1087. The priory was built outside the walls of the town, and this is perhaps why Gerald did not stay in the priory but preferred the greater security and comfort of the castle.

St Mary's Sanctuary dates from the twelfth century, but little from that period remains. The main structure dates from the fourteenth century, from the time of John de Hastings, the Lord of Gavenny. There is a medieval font dating from the twelfth century though this is now on a Victorian base and covered by a canopy of the same period. There is much to be seen in the Priory that is later than Gerald's time, in particular many fine monuments and sculptures. Amongst the many artefacts there is a fifteenth-century wooden carving of Jesse, which formerly served as the base for a family tree depicting the line from Jesse to Jesus Christ, a wooden tomb fissure of Sir John de Hastings (1326) together with wooden panelling, and several tombs of the Hastings and Herbert families spanning the period from the 1300 to the early 1500s. Many of the monuments deserve close attention, not least for their historical interest, and most are in reasonable condition despite a certain amount of defacement during the Commonwealth period. Also there are two reconstructed tombs, one of an unknown lady of the Hastings family and the other of Eva de Braose, a familiar name, whose hands hold a small casket denoting a 'heart burial'.

This custom of the separate burial of the heart apparently commenced during the first Crusade, as the heart, which was regarded as the centre of the body controlling affection, was often sent to a favourite place or to a favourite person to be buried in memory of the deceased. The practicality of this probably played a part, as it was easier to embalm a heart and consign it to a lead case for transmission, whereas transportation of the whole body would have given rise to much greater problems.

Perhaps one of the most famous 'heart burials' is that of Robert the Bruce (king of Scotland, 1272-1329). He requested that his heart be taken to, and buried in, the Holy Land, as he had vowed to go to fight before Jerusalem. Sadly, the carrier of the heart was himself slain on the way, and so the heart was returned to Scotland and buried at Melrose abbey, where it remains.

In the close proximity of the priory is a medieval tithe barn which has recently been restored and is the home for a magnificent and large modern tapestry. This depicts the landscape around Abergavenny and the various historic events that have taken place in the area over the 1000 years to the millennium year of 2000. Sadly, Gerald's journey is not one of the scenes, although the massacre of the Welsh by William de Braose is there for posterity. It took five years to complete the tapestry, which is an outstanding example of the craftsmanship of over sixty stitchers and a reminder that the old skills have not vanished. The barn is now a museum and restaurant.

Abergavenny was obviously a lively town in Gerald's time and is still so this day, with its shops and old buildings together with the tower of the town hall dominating the centre, but the calm of the ruins of the castle and the peace of the priory remind us firmly of Gerald's passing by.

Chapter 5
Usk and Caerleon

The road from Abergavenny drops down through the widening valley of the Usk and its beautiful countryside, with the Black Mountains fading into the distance behind the traveller, until we finally reach Usk itself and its castle. Way over to the left of the valley road stand the remains of Raglan castle, a formidable military castle not built until 1435, some 250 years after Gerald's time – and indeed some 200 years after Edward I's huge fortresses of Wales such as Caernarfon and Conwy. It was mainly built as a statement of wealth rather than military power, although it came into its own militarily in the Civil War when it withstood in 1646 one of the longest sieges of the War. It was subsequently demolished by Cromwell's men. Even so it is a very fine example of a late medieval castle-cum-palace in Britain.

At Usk castle Gerald tells us that a large number of men were signed with the cross following a sermon by Archbishop Baldwin and an address by William, Bishop of Llandaff, the Archdeacon of Bangor acting as interpreter. Gerald states that a large number of those converted were criminals convicted of robbery and murder. It must have been one way to escape from the results of their crimes to perhaps a better life despite the privations of medieval warfare. Coincidentally there is still a large prison in Usk, visible from the castle ramparts, but the offer of taking the cross and going on a Crusade is no longer an available method of avoiding sentences! One can imagine the sermons being given before the Great Keep of the castle. This was constructed in stone by Richard 'Strongbow' de Clare in about 1170. Before that date there may have been a wooden motte-and-bailey castle, and the castle Gerald would have seen would have been primarily of wood construction. At least, one must assume this to have been the case as most of the stone structures, still extant, are dated from a later period: for example, Gilbert de Clare's Treasure Tower, built in 1289. This tower housed a 'dog called Coker' which may well be the first reference to a Cocker spaniel! The central grass area of the present castle is well patronised by hens, ducks and geese, all free range, as they would have been centuries ago.

This central area is next to the Great Hall which dates from the early 1300s, as do most of the still visible walls. The entire castle dominates the town of Usk which was itself built on the Roman fort of Burrium.

Looking down from the battlements one can see the parish church of St Mary's which was originally the church of Usk Priory. The priory, which was founded in about 1160 by the Benedictines, housed an abbess and nuns of noble birth. It contains several memorials. One is to the Welsh chronicler Adam of Usk, who died in 1420, and it is said to bear the oldest Welsh-language epitaph. Another commemorates Walter Jones, an Elizabethan soldier who died in 1656. Outside the west porch is the gravestone of a Jesuit priest, St David Lewis, who was executed nearby in 1679, reminding us of the difficulties of religious life in those days.

The road down to Caerleon follows the curves of the Usk, passing on the left the pretty church of Llanbadog and the island of the same name.

The town of Caerleon is renowned for the extensive remains of the occupation by the Roman legionaries and the Roman domination of the area. Today the ruins and excavations are impressive, but it is easy to forget that when Gerald visited Caerleon they were far more impressive as it was a mere 800 years since the Romans had left the country towards the end of the fourth century.

As in so many other towns, much of the masonry was subsequently used to build the medieval houses after the Romans left, but the ruins were still buildings of some magnitude in 1188. Gerald writes that he could still see remains of the long-lost splendour of the fortress. In particular:

> This city was of undoubted antiquity, and handsomely built of brick by the Romans; many vestiges of its former splendour may yet be seen. Immense palaces, ornamented with gilded roofs, in imitation of Roman magnificence; a tower of prodigious size, remarkable hot baths, relics of temples, and theatres inclosed within fine walls, parts of which remain standing. You will find on all sizes, both within and without the walls, subterranean vaults and aqueducts; and what I think worthy of notice, stoves contrived with wonderful art, to transmit the heat insensibly through narrow tubes.

From this it would seem that, even with a little romanticism on Gerald's behalf, quite a considerable number of buildings were still standing, particularly around the fortress baths, and that some of the basilica at the baths was extant.

Today, little exists above ground level, but with the benefit of excellent excavations one can see clearly the amphitheatre standing as it does outside the ditch and mound of the old defensive walls. A substantial part of one of the four barrack areas has been uncovered. Probably of greatest interest are the remains of the huge fortress bath, preserved under cover, which enabled each member of the XX Legion to swim or bath at least once a week. The fortress is a huge testimony to the power of the Roman occupation and would, at its peak, have housed some 5,500 armed infantry with all the necessary services, staff, wives and others. There is much to see and many of the remains of the treasures to which Gerald alluded are kept in the Legionary Museum at the centre of the old fortress itself. If one stands in the middle of the amphitheatre or tarries quietly at the baths, with only a little imagination one can envisage the Caerleon of Gerald and, with only a little leap in time, hear the crowds and feel the hustle and bustle of Roman legionaries at their Isca camp going about their business.

The Caerleon of Gerald's time must have been a busy town. He points out that it is beautifully situated on the Usk and that, when the tide came in, it was navigable for ships. He also tells that in his time there was a soothsayer called Meilyr, who inhabited Caerleon. He was made mad for several years as, when he was making love to a beautiful girl he had fancied for a long time, she suddenly turned into a hideous hag, which seems rather bad luck for Meilyr. However, when his wits returned he was able to tell the future through his familiarity with unclean spirits. (Gerald wryly remarks that not always was his information reliable!) He saw these spirits mainly near religious houses and could always tell when someone was lying as he saw demons dancing on the liar's tongue. He could also recognise any false monk, but sometimes he became overwrought with the volume of the spirits. The good news was that if a copy of St John's Gospel was put on his lap the spirits fled and he was alright again, for the time being at least.

Most of Meilyr's insights seemed to have involved sex. He foresaw the downfall of Enoch, the then Abbot of Strata Marcella, who ran away from his monastery with a nun. He discussed with Cynan, Abbot of Whitland, how he, Meilyr, had been observing the activities of a certain woman, at which the good abbot broke down and admitted lusting after her, for which he was duly mortified.

On a more political note Meilyr, through an incubus (a demon in male form), advised Hywel ab Iorwerth. Hywel feared that King Henry II was going to take vengeance because of his ravaging in Wales. Meilyr told him that he did not need to worry as Henry would turn his attention to beating the French, which indeed happened, and that Hywel would thus be unmolested. Finally he advised the same Hywel that in the future, in 1174, he would be wounded at Usk Castle, but not killed, and would escape alive. One wonders whether Meilyr had offered his two predictions to Hywel on the basis 'do you want the good news or the bad news first?'! Ironically, Meilyr was wrong in one detail because it was he himself who was wounded at Usk and who died soon after. As Gerald said, he was not always reliable in his forecasts. Indeed Gerald seems quite sceptical as he does not believe that spirits can be seen by one person but by not another. However, despite that, the story of Meilyr was one he deemed worth telling.

Gerald continued on his journey, commenting that he had passed Monmouth castle and the Forest of Dean a long way to their left. The Forest supplied both venison and iron ore, and later also oak for shipbuilding as, Hoare tells us, 'The oak of this forest was very considerable, that it was said to have been part of the instructions of the Spanish Armada to destroy the timber of this place.' The party carried on down toward the Severn estuary approaching Newport.

Chapter 6
Newport and Cardiff

Gerald reports that at Newport many people were convinced to take the cross. The number implies that Newport and the area must have been fairly populous. During his journey to date through the various market towns and countryside Gerald would still have been able to identify with some recognisable features of his time. But if he had come to the present day south Wales, with its indus-trialisation, population and sheer mass of buildings he would have been dumbstruck, and he would have been further overwhelmed during his journey through Cardiff, on past the Port Talbot steelworks near Margam abbey and the industrial area of Neath. Still, despite the massive changes, there would have been some connections to memories of his day. He would have seen the Wentloog, named after Gwynllyw, who we shall meet later, which he crossed between Newport and Cardiff. He describes it as a muddy marshland criss-crossed by hollows in its bed caused by the waters running down to the Severn and the action of the incoming sea. The Wentloog is still there, but the crossing is no longer by fords but by winding roads with the ever-visible industrial estates inland. But looking out to the Severn the view must have been much the same then, although the fact that the marshland is now a bird protection area might have surprised Gerald, as it must have been teeming with wildlife in his time.

He talks of a ford in the Wentloog called Rhyd Pencarn where, in his day the public highway ran, but now is no longer visible. He quotes a saying of Merlin Sylvester, the Merlin of King Arthur's legend, that if a strong freckled man were to come to the ford and pass over it the Welsh will be beaten. Sure enough Gerald informs us that Henry II in 1163 was going to pass over a new ford, but such was the commotion of buglers and trumpeters to welcome him at the crossing, that his horse bolted and he rushed to and crossed by the old ford. As Henry was both strong and freckled, the prophecy was fulfilled and Rhys ap Gruffudd surrendered to him in due course. This was possibly an example of too much Welsh hospitality and enthusiasm, as had the welcome been more muted his horse would not have bolted and history might have been different.

The party probably stayed at least one night (Sunday 13 March) and possibly two at Newport Castle. The remains of the new castle overlooking the Usk are mainly overbuilt with the development of roads but there are some small remnants of the buildings from between 1327 and 1386. But this is long after Gerald's visit. The castle he saw was probably an earlier motte-and-bailey construction on the

Capital, Newport

top of Stow Hill where the cathedral of St Woolos is now found. Nothing exists of the castle, which would have overlooked the town of Newport from the ridge above it and the river and sea. But in St Woolos there are several pre-conquest and Norman remains. The former are limited to stone foundations and the frame of an early door which now doubles as a cupboard. There is a magnificent Norman arch built on tapering pillars, which are quoted as coming from the ruins of Caerleon, the arch being sculpted with symbols relating to baptism. The base of the font and the pillars in the aisles also date from that time. The aisles and the chancel are attractively and unusually skewed at an angle to each other. At the east end, above the altar, there is a magnificent modern painted canvas mural and window designed by John Piper in the 1960s which sits well with the architecture of the ancient cathedral.

There are many items of interest spanning the centuries. It is of a particular interest to students of democracy that in the cathedral yard is a monument recalling that on 4 November 1839 twenty supporters of the Chartist movement died of shots in Newport and that ten of the victims are buried in unmarked graves in the churchyard. It will be recalled that the Chartist movement was key to the development of the working classes and their freedom in early Victorian Britain. The ruling classes regarded the Chartists as dangerous political radicals, even revolutionaries. Their Charter was a petition to Parliament asserting the rights of the ordinary people for freedom to work and to be adequately remunerated. The Establishment saw the movement as so dangerous that Queen Victoria herself was moved to the Isle of Wight so that her safety, in the light of the unrest, could be secured. In the end, as evidenced by the memorial in Newport, the movement was suppressed by force.

Font, St Woolo's, Newport

The name Woolo is intriguing. History relates that the saint built his original church, probably in wattle and daub. This is where the present entrance chapel is sited. The original church was built in about 500 so the foundation goes back a long way. In fact the saint, a Welsh chieftain, was called Gundleus, or in Welsh Gwynllyw, which has been anglicised to Woolo, though quite how this transformation occurred defeats imagination. He obviously led quite a life with his wife Gwladys, so legend has it, and their married life started off in high form as his potential father-in-law, St Brychan of Brecknock, refused to sanction the marriage. So Gundleus kidnapped Gwladys and married her! It is alleged that he was aided and abetted in this by King Arthur, who also rather fancied Gwladys! After their marriage they lived a life of riot, banditry and violence until their first son, who was to become St Cadog, told them to settle down, which they promptly did. Gundleus and Gwladys were thus converted and decided to lead an ascetic life. It is recorded that St Gwladys and St Woolo, after their conversion and as part of their austere life, used to bathe nightly in the Usk and followed this by a mile long walk along the banks of the Usk in the nude! Cadog managed after a while to convince them to stop the practice and separate! So far as the church is concerned the legend holds that St Woolo dreamt that he should search for a white ox with a black spot on its forehead and build his church where he found it. This presumably is what he did and we now have the most beautiful small cathedral at Stow Hill. Gwladys and Cadog made their own ecclesiastical marks elsewhere in Wales.

St Cadog seems to have been a bit of a prig, denying his mother and father their fun but he seems to share his father's predilection with cattle. At one time he sheltered or gave sanctuary to a man who had killed three of King Arthur's soldiers. Arthur demanded of him that he should give 300 best oxen to him to recompense him. Arthur insisted that the oxen should be multi-coloured. Cadog agreed and when they passed before him the oxen changed to the colour which Arthur had demanded. However as soon as Arthur's men touched the cattle they, the cattle, turned into bundles of fern. Immediately Arthur asked forgiveness and extended St Cadog's right of sanctuary, at which point the ferns turned back to oxen and were all safely transported to their own stalls. St Cadog was obviously not a saint to be messed around with! He also seems to have had irrevocable means of punishment as twice he caused his enemies to be swallowed up in the ground. He had the power to raise the dead, as he did in two instances.

From Newport, the party moved on to Cardiff and probably stayed the night at the castle. Even in Gerald's day the castle must have been an impressive sight as he refers to events in 1158, some thirty years earlier, when the castle was fortified by a circle of very high walls, and these walls were guarded by a huge squad of sentinels, at least 120 men-at-arms and a great number of archers. Even so the walls were scaled at that time by the Welsh leader Ifor Bach, and the Earl of Gloucester and his wife and child were captured.

The site of the castle goes back to Roman times when a ten acre site was constructed but such remains as existed were incorporated into a typical motte-and-bailey Norman castle in 1091. During the twelfth century the fortress was reinforced with stone and the twelve-sided shell keep was constructed. This still stands, giving us in the twenty-first century a superb example of how things would have looked in Gerald's day. Also there are significant ruins of the great wall which separated the inner and outer wards of the Norman castle, all within the walls of the Roman fortifications. These presumably are the fortifications to which Gerald refers, even though the Welsh caused much damage to the fabric in 1183–1184, when they revolted against the dominance of their English masters.

Building a castle

Nevertheless Hoare opines that in the days of Gerald, the castle was probably in a high state of preservation. Now the castle is much changed around the existing central Norman keep. This has occurred over many years, but more specifically through alterations by the Bute family, who made extensive modifications to the exterior of the castle. The First Marquis of Bute employed 'Capability' Brown to landscape the grounds. He removed a huge ward wall between the inner and outer courts and several ancient buildings to create a scene more 'fitting' to contemporary taste. In particular the whimsical approach of the third Marquis of Bute, who began the castle's rebirth in 1865 with typical Victorian drive for innovation, has left its mark for posterity, and the highly decorative rooms include an Arab room and hall and various bedrooms.

The clock tower, which was built in between 1869 and 1874, stands high above Cardiff in all its pseudo-continental style and dominates the nearby impressive local government buildings. These buildings (mostly Edwardian) constitute what is regarded as one of the most impressive civic centres in Europe and are a fine example of twentieth-century renaissance style, reflecting Welsh national pride in its institutions, and the naissance of its aspirations for the future. Among the buildings located there are Cardiff City Hall, the National Museum and Gallery of Wales, the County Law Courts, the Central Police Station, and part of Cardiff University.

Gerald may have been impressed with the Cardiff of his day, but the recent changes to the Bay area, including the Welsh Assembly Building and the Millennium Stadium, would surely have impressed him even more. However, with his knowledge of Wales, and its churches and the arena at Caerleon, he might well have taken all these changes into his stride. The castle, and Museum of Wales and the city itself deserve a far longer stay than the day Gerald allowed himself before moving on to the cathedral at Llandaff. However, in his book he relates a story about Henry II who stayed the night at Cardiff in 1172 and this may well be the precursor of the British attitudes to Sunday observance! He was confronted by a man in a white habit who stated:

> Christ and His Holy Mother, John the Baptist and the Apostle Peter salute thee, and command thee strictly to prohibit throughout thy whole dominions every kind of buying and selling on Sundays; and not to suffer any work to be done on those days, except such as relates to the preparation of daily food; that due attention may be paid to the performance of the divine offices. If thou dost this, all thy undertakings shall be successful, and thou shalt lead a happy life.

The king was unimpressed and sadly did not follow the advice, as many misfortunes befell him the following year. One wonders what would have happened if Sunday observance had come into Wales at that time.

Gerald refers to Barry Island, just off the Cardiff coast, as Barry, or Barri, was his family name. It sounds as though the island of his day would have been a peaceful place. He tells the story that there was a crack in a rock at the landing place through which you could hear a noise like blacksmiths at work. One view as to how these were produced is that there were fairies, or spirits of the mountains, constantly employed hammering in creating a brazen wall, intended by the prophet Merlin for the perpetual defence of Britain. Also Merlin was alleged to have had an affair with some beautiful ladies and became forgetful of them, with the result that they were doomed by the laws of magic to continue their hammering until he regained his power and freedom. Sadly the development of Barry with its harbour and heavy industry, and as a seaside resort, makes his time seem a long way away. There are many changes taking place on the island but it will be some time before it achieves the glory of times past. The remains of a chapel dedicated to St Baruch still remain and Gerald refers to this as his ivy-clad chapel. St Baruch was a disciple of St Cadog, but little is known of him. Hoare mentions that on the island there were:

> burrow ducks, from the circumstances of their making their nests in the rabbit holes . . . Towards the southern part of the island, on a spot called Nell's Point, is a fine well to which great numbers of women resort on Holy Tuesday, and having washed their eyes at the spring, each drops a pin in it. The landlord of the boarding house [on the island] told me, that in cleaning out the well, he took out a pint full of these votive pins.

Chapter 7
The See of Llandaff, and Margam Abbey

Gerald tells us that on the next morning after their stay in Cardiff they preached at Llandaff, probably at the site of the present cross on Cathedral Green. Gerald states that the English stood on one side and the Welsh on the other, and that many from both nations took the cross. Gerald must have felt a bit like a referee between the Welsh and the Normans, with his feet being slightly in two camps as he was descended from both Marcher lords and Welsh princes. 'He was proud of his Welsh royal blood; prouder still of being a Marcher – one of the select band of pioneers who 'inherit our courage from the Welsh and our skill in warfare from the Normans" (*A Mirror of Medieval Wales*).

A cross still stands on the green and it is possible that part of it could date back to Gerald's time.

They stayed the night of Monday 14 March with William de Salso Marisco, the local Bishop, and Archbishop Baldwin celebrated Mass the following morning. The gates to the old Bishop's castle overlook the green. The cathedral itself is in a valley slightly below the level of the green rather than on a high point but the steeple and tower, both of a much later date than Gerald, dominate the area. The cathedral which Gerald visited must nevertheless have been impressive. Its building began under the first Norman Bishop, Urban, in 1120. There had been a church or churches beforehand but all that remains of those precursors is a Celtic cross, which is now by the entrance to the chapter house.

The cathedral is dedicated to Saint Teilo, who was said to have been Archbishop in the sixth century. It is reputed that St Teilo had three bodies, or rather that three bodies of the saint were discovered the day after his death. Even in the days when relics were very important this seems an unlikely story and was probably invented to account for the fact that the churches at Llandaff, Llandeilo Fawr, and Penally, all claimed to possess his body. Doubtless at his death his relics were distributed far and wide, not only in Wales but also in Brittany where there are churches dedicated to him, and in monuments and memorials he is not infrequently seen as riding on a stag. The dedication of twelve churches in the present Anglican Diocese of St David's, and of six in that of Llandaff, also show they owe their origin to the zeal with which his relics were distributed. However, the cathedral still boasts the reputed skull of St Teilo, mounted on an art noveau silver base, though sadly the skull has been dated by experts only to the thirteenth century!

The cathedral itself is very imposing and is dominated by the statue of 'Christ in Majesty' by Sir Jacob Epstein which was installed on the organ case on the pulpitum in 1957. Despite its modernity it contrasts well with the rest of the ancient architecture although some regard it as too dominant. Much of the past has survived despite neglect and substantial damage during the Second World War (1939–1945). For example the Urban arch behind the High Altar was built in around 1170, as was St Teilo's door, both of which would have been in existence at Gerald's visit. The St Teilo door now leads to a modern processional way and to St David's Chapel, which is the chapel of The Royal Regiment of Wales. In the chapel the battle honours of the regiment and its history are represented in a peaceful surround. Again the south door dates back to 1120 but the area of the choir and the nave are from the early thirteenth century, as indeed is the centre part of the west front, the Chapter House and a fair proportion of the fabric. There are many artefacts of interest including, amongst several effigies, that of St Teilo. The Lady Chapel was built in about

1280 when William de Braose was Bishop (1266–1287). He presumably was descended from the William de Braose we met earlier, and his effigy lies to the north side of the altar. There is an ancient squint and there are several more modern pieces from the pre-Raphaelite art movement in window glass dating from the 1860s, contributed by Rossetti, William Morris and Burne-Jones. In all there are many contrasts within the cathedral but it remains a cohesive whole, both architecturally and aesthetically.

Leaving Llandaff after the morning service the party passed on to Margam abbey passing through Ewenni where Gerald mentions there was a little cell. He does not seem to have rested at, or indeed thought particularly highly of, Ewenni, as no doubt he wished to press on to what was obviously the great Cistercian house at Margam. But to tarry awhile at Ewenni is time well spent, as the church is a wonderful and well-preserved Norman building. It is a fine specimen of a fortified ecclesiastical building protected by strong curtain walls and gates.

The church's former beauty has been captured in a painting of 'The Transept of Ewenny Priory' by the great British painter J. M. W. Turner in about 1797, which now hangs in the National Museum of Wales, Cardiff. In Turner's time it appears to have been in some disrepair and his painting depicts a lady feeding her chickens in the church! Nowadays the Priory is beautifully maintained and shows its own beauty for itself.

The Priory was founded somewhere between 1115 and 1120 by William de Londres. On his tomb is inscribed in Latin *'Ici gist Morice de Lundres le fundur Deu li rende sun labor. AM'* which translates as 'Here lies Maurice de Londres, the Founder. God reward him for his work.' As well as being the founder, Maurice was somewhat of a 'bounder', having robbed the church at Llandaff and generally plundered and killed itinerant merchants at Llandaff. Perhaps his denunciation and threatened excommunication by Pope Honorius II in 1128 concentrated his mind suitably, causing him to mend his ways. The house was that of the Benedictine order and originally had a complement of twelve monks and a prior. The approach to the Priory is along the side of a twelfth-century curtain wall, tower and gatehouse extended in the next century, which now encloses the private residence and gardens of the Turberville family, long associated with Ewenni. The church itself is outside the walls and has been altered over the years, but much of the original remains.

On one of the nave pillars a painting can still be made out which dates from about 1140. Some of the old windows remain, but others have been altered to increase the light to the interior. The font predates the church and the church is split by the pulpitum screen that would have split the monks from the congregation. The screen was probably erected in the thirteenth century and is now surmounted by a glass screen erected in 2006, the work of a Swansea-based artist, Alexander Beleschenko, blending the old with the new. Past the pulpitum is the monastic end of the priory and some of the original tiles can be seen. Amongst various stoneworks a carving from the twelfth century, an eleventh-century carved cross and various tomb slabs remain. Between the transept and the presbytery is an oak screen dating from the fourteenth century, whilst the presbytery itself is a good example of twelfth-century barrel vaulting and cross-vaulting. Wall paintings from the 1140s survive. Originally the whole would have been brightly and completely coloured, as indeed would have been all the priories in Gerald's era.

The road onward to Margam passes the huge Port Talbot steelworks, a very different view to that which Gerald would have enjoyed, of sandy beaches and the hills around the coast. Sadly the old Margam abbey has largely gone but its remains are in Margam park. It is a just a small fragment of what was once the richest monastic house in Wales, and this is possibly why Gerald and Baldwin hurried to enjoy the hospitality afforded by the Cistercian monks. Indeed Gerald tells us that Margam was:

> more celebrated for its charitable deeds than any other of that order in Wales. On this account it is an undoubted fact that, as a reward for that abundant charity which the monastery had always, in times of need, exercised towards strangers and poor persons, in a season of an approaching famine, their corn and provisions were perceptibly, by divine assistance, increased, like the widow's cruise of oil, by the means of the prophet Elijah.

In Gerald's time there was a serious famine prompting the monks to decide to buy food from Bristol. They sent off a boat to collect the supplies but it did not return. However, a nearby field was found to be miraculously producing crops, even though it was not the right season. So there was sufficient food to feed the starving, and through such events Margam abbey's reputation continued to flourish. Gerald relates some other stories about Margam. In the early days of the abbey, a young Welshman laid claim to some of Margam's land, and pursued his claims without success until he was inspired by the devil to burn down one of the abbey barns which was full of corn. Needless to say he went mad and was bound in chains, from which he escaped. He arrived at the gatehouse screaming that he was being burnt up inside by the monks. He died miserably shortly after. Another man struck a fellow guest in the Refectory and was

Chapter House, Margam

found dead in the morning at the very same spot where he had given offence. So Margam was a place of hospitality, miracles and retribution.

A plaque shows how the layout of the priory would have been and there are a few remains. The polygonal chapter house and one of the outbuildings can be seen.

You can still see the size and layout of the abbey itself, the present church only taking up half the size of the old one. At the dissolution of the abbey under Henry VIII in 1536, Sir Rice Mansel took possession of Margam on the King's behalf. He subsequently leased the property and in 1540 bought the buildings and secured most of the abbey's possessions using them to build a huge rambling mansion which must have incorporated much of the stonework of the abbey buildings themselves.

The whole area is now dominated by a large Tudor Gothic Mansion known as Margam Castle, built by

Christopher Rice Mansel Talbot in 1830–1840, and so the fine abbey that Gerald knew moved on to become the old house and then Margam Castle.

No doubt the hospitality of the abbey carried on in the new buildings and visitors were made comfortable and lived in a convivial way over the years. The old stones of Margam had moved to these new functions and sites, a fate which affected many similar medieval structures which were torn down to be incorporated in a new location, and the Mansell and Talbot families moved into the abbey with fine tombs and memorials left for posterity. This is a juxtaposition of history often seen.

Gerald in his book strays away from Margam into giving his views about dogs. He regards the dog as man's best friend, who is prepared to die for his owner in all circumstances. He relates two stories from the classics to illustrate the bravery of dogs in defence of their masters. In one of these he tells of the death of Cadwallon, who murdered his brother Owain to inherit the estates owned by his father, Caradog ap Iestin. God caught up with Cadwallon as he was crushed to pieces by a castle wall, which he and his family had assaulted. Owain, however, had a very fine greyhound who had defended his master whilst being pierced with arrows and spears, and he lived to show his scars and tell the tale.

In Gerald's experience a dog is more reliant on its nose than its eyes and when he loses his master he can tell from the smell on his master's clothes whether he can be fully sure he has the right man. Also a dog has a healing property in its tongue, unlike, says Gerald, the wolf, which only infect wounds with his tongue rather than healing them.

When Gerald extols the bravery and loyalty of dogs it is perhaps surprising that he does not relate the story concerning one of his contemporaries Prince Llywelyn ap

Iorwerth (The Great) (d.1240). He was said to have a hunting place at Beddgelert in north Wales. He went off on a hunting trip and left his infant son in the protection of his faithful greyhound. When he returned he was greeted by the dog, its muzzle and body soaked in blood. Llywelyn rushed into the nursery to find the child's cradle overturned and blood everywhere, but of his son there was no sign. He thought his dog had eaten the child. In anguish he plunged his sword into the dog – only to hear shortly after a baby's cry. To his astonishment he found not only his sleeping son, but also the dead body of a huge wolf which had been killed by Gelert in a massive fight. Llywelyn then went back to his faithful greyhound which licked his hand as it gently expired. The prince was so upset that he erected a tomb over the body of his dog Gelert, and this can still be seen in a field at Beddgelert with a slab lying on its side and two upright stones as a continual memory. It is alleged that an old Welsh proverb comes from this history: '*Mor edifar a'r dyn a drywanodd ei filgi*' (As penitent as the man who slew his greyhound).

This incident occurred after 1188, but Gerald would surely have heard of it before finishing his book. Or perhaps the story is a mere fabrication by villagers of Beddgelert in the late eighteenth or early nineteenth century to encourage walking tourists, like the Reverend William Bingley, to visit Beddgelert – although the name of the village might also be a reference to St Celert or Celer. Either way it is a touching tale exemplifying the faithfulness of dogs.

One thing is certain: in the animal life of Beddgelert there is a bear, Rupert by name, who was immortalised in a comic strip written and illustrated there by an inhabitant of the village, Alfred Bestall!

Chapter 8
Passage over the rivers Avon and Neath, and then Swansea and Gower

It is left to our imagination as to how different the hazards of Gerald's journey would be from those of the present day. At least he did not have to put up with traffic jams and congestion. He would have been travelling in the pure air of the 1100s and not the polluted atmosphere of nowadays. Needless to say the smells of the countryside and his companions must have been very different and, in terms of bodily hygiene, not very acceptable to the modern nose. Nevertheless his journey must have been long and fraught and he would have been subject to the vagaries of the weather from which the modern traveller, sitting in a car, is sheltered. He does mention from time to time various hazards which must have been tougher than normal for him and his party, for example (see Chapter 4) how they passed down a rugged pass on a narrow track overgrown with trees at Coed Gwythne.

From Margam abbey Gerald no doubt would have taken the old Roman road following the coastline, which would have been for once quite an easy route. The Roman road itself is now well buried under the A48. As Gerald's party approached the rivers Avon and Neath he gives us a little glimpse of the problems of the journey in 1188 as he alludes to the problems and hazards of moving along a sandy shore with an incoming tide. The Avon was successfully forded but the party was delayed for a time by the ebbing tide.

The next trial was to be the crossing over the Neath:

which, on account of its quicksands, is the most

dangerous and inaccessible in South Wales. A pack-horse belonging to the author, which had proceeded by the lower way near the sea, although in the midst of many others, was the only one which sunk down into the abyss.

In the event the animal was saved but not without some difficulty and danger to Gerald's servants. Gerald himself suffered some damage to his books and baggage which could not have helped his temper. This must have been fairly traumatic to him when one considers the value and time of investment in the actual writing and the scripting of the books, not forgetting the problems of composition. Each book was unique and not a printed book as we would know it, as the printing process was not introduced into Europe until some 300 years later. He does not complain as to his losses or the size of them, but merely tells us that they came to the river after several upsets and danger and 'the alarm occasioned by this unusual kind of road, made us hasten our steps over the quicksands, in opposition to the advice of our guide, and fear quickened our pace; whereas, through these difficult passages, as we there learned, the proceeding should be with moderate speed'.One can imagine the consternation and worry of the party. There was more difficulty to come: it was not easy to ford the Neath as the passage of the ford changed at each tide, making it difficult to find the new line of the fords after heavy rains when the river was swollen and flooded.

Gerald comments on a problem his uncle David II, Bishop of Wales, had when trying to cross the same ford in inclement weather. He asked a local chaplain who was an expert in the crossing but who gloried in the unusual name, for a man of the cloth, of Rhydderch the Liar, to assist him. Rhydderch jumped on David's horse, which was obviously a very good one, and rode off into the woods and would not return until he was promised that his recent suspension from his office as chaplain was restored. This was duly done, together with suitable monetary compensation, so the horse was returned and all was well, with David presumably fording the Neath satisfactorily. No doubt Rhydderch retained his nickname.

However, Gerald avoided this particular difficulty of the ford by crossing by boat. This was presumably at Bretton Ferry.

Gerald crossed the river leaving the diocese of Llandaff and entering that of St David's and passed near the monastery of Neath to his right. The monastery must have been clearly visible to the party then; the buildings are now in the centre of an industrial estate. The abbey was founded in 1129 and was originally a house of the order of Savigny, a Benedictine order, but it merged in 1147 with the Cistercian order, making it one of the oldest Cistercian houses in Wales. It became one of the most powerful and presumably richest houses in Wales and its early buildings were reconstructed in the thirteenth and fourteenth centuries. Leland comments that 'It semid to me the fairest abbay of al Wales.'

The wealth of the house was much enhanced by the commercial enterprise of the monks as they traded across the Bristol Channel on their own behalf. This they did through the control they had over the abbey quays, which, being outside the jurisdiction of Neath itself, enabled them to undercut the port of Neath and by so doing boost their own trade and those who sailed from their quays. The church was always able to employ capitalistic concepts. The abbey must have been a fine sight in Gerald's time and subsequently, although now in ruins. Much of the outline of the main church remains, as do a number of the outbuildings in the west range and one can imagine the monks wending their way down the remains of an old stairway from the dormitory to the various services in the abbey. In part of the buildings is a mansion, which was built in the mid 1500s by Sir Richard Williams who acquired the site after the Dissolution in 1539. This must have been quite an impressive private house. This passed to Sir John Herbert and was occupied throughout the 1600s. The house is built above a thirteenth-century undercroft, which was once the monks' dormitory, with nearby latrines. One or two fragments of monuments and some of the original tiling have been collected. Later the abbey served part of its life as a copper works and foundry and in a way there is symmetry in its development considering it is now located in the industrial area.

Gerald passed the abbey by, possibly because he wanted to get to Swansea quickly, particularly after the trauma of the river crossings, and no doubt he had visited it on other occasions. The ruins of Neath abbey are well worth a short visit, even though marked by the passing of time and the industrial revolution, and even though the world seems to have forgotten them.

So the party reached Swansea on Thursday 17 March, and spent the night in Swansea castle. The castle was, as were so many in Gerald's time, of the motte-and-bailey style, and nothing of it remains above ground. The new castle, which replaced it and its successor, dates from the late thirteenth century. It is surrounded nowadays by roads and modern buildings but still stands on the edge of the cliff over looking the Tawe in a highly strategic position.

In the evening two monks were overheard by Gerald talking about the day that had passed and the dangers in which they had been involved. Gerald says that one monk referred to the country they had passed through as a hard country whilst the other disagreed saying that it was a soft country, the first relating to the barrenness of the countryside whilst the other, the quick-sands.

The following morning Mass was said and many were persuaded to take the cross. However one man, Cador, who was elderly, approached the Archbishop and, with tears in his eyes, gave Baldwin one tenth of his worldly wealth as he felt he was too infirm to go on the Crusade in person, requesting Baldwin to remit half the penance he would otherwise incur. This was agreed and then Cador returned and said to the Archbishop that he really did want to go on the Crusade but if the Archbishop would remit the entire penance he would double his cash contribution. Baldwin presumably accepted as Gerald says that he smiled and put his arms around Cador, admiring both his devoutness and ingenuity in avoiding taking the cross. So there were ways of avoiding the hazards of the Crusades by financial means and the shrewd Cador managed to hold on to eighty per cent of his wealth. No doubt it would have cost a lot more if he had actually signed up, as absentee lords' properties could fall into disrepair or worse!

At St Mary's church in Swansea there is reference to the Crusades and Crusaders in a fifteenth-century resurrection brass remembering Sir Hugh Johnys and his wife, Dame Maud, their five sons and four daughters. The inscription was recorded by Hoare as:

> Pray for the sowle of Sir Hugh Johnys, Kinght, and Dame Mawde, his wife, whych Sir Hugh was made knight at the Holy Sepulcre of our Lord Jhu Christ in the City of Jerusalem the XIII day of August the yere of oure Lord Gode MCCCCXLI and the said Sir Hugh had contynuwd in the Waris ther' long tyme before by space of fyve yer that is to say ageynst the

Turkis and Sarsyns in the Pties of Troy Grecie and Turky under John yt time Emproure of Constantyneople and after that was Knight Marshall of Ffraunce under John Duke of Som'set by the space of ffive yere, and in likewise aftyr that was Knight Marshall of Ingland under the good John Duke of Norfolke, which John made unty hym the Manor of Landymo' to hym and to his heyre', for ev'more upon whose soulhs Jhu have mercy.

He seems to have had a very full life.

Gerald tells the story of a strange happening which had been rumoured to have occurred some time before in the Swansea area. One can imagine Gerald telling this and other stories round the fire to while away the March Thursday evening they stayed in Swansea. He was, as we have seen, renowned for his good company and conversation. He attributes his story to a priest, so it must be true!

When he was a young innocent child of twelve, the priest Elidyr ran away to avoid the strictures of his teacher and hid by the bank of a river for two days without any food. Two very small men appeared and said that if he followed them they would take him away to a land where all was pleasure and fun. This he did and followed them through a long dark tunnel to an Eldorado where the countryside was so beautiful – although the skies were dark and the days appeared overcast as there was no sun, and the nights pitch black as there was neither moon nor stars. He was taken to meet the king who was amazed at what he saw and handed him over to his son to look after. The world was one in miniature, no-one lied or cheated, they did not eat meat or fish and survived on milk dishes and when they visited the real world from time to time, they would return contemptuous of the ways of humans in the upper world.

Elidyr used to return home, at first accompanied and then, when he was trusted, alone. He told no-one of his experiences except his mother. She asked him to bring her back a present of gold from the subterranean world and so he stole a golden ball and then rushed home to present it to his mother. He rushed so fast, with the little men in pursuit, that when he arrived home he tripped over the doorstep, dropped the ball, and this was seized by the little men who showed to him every form of contempt, derision and scorn. Elidyr realised with great shame all that he had done and that what his mother had asked was wrong, so he headed back, presumably to apologise for his actions, but the tunnel had vanished and although he searched for the entrance for many a year he never found it or the subterranean land again. Eventually he returned to his family, studies and life and subsequently became a priest, but he would always burst into tears when telling the tale, even though he could still remember the language of the little folk, which Gerald tells us was very like Greek!

Gerald wonders whether the folk tale is true and does not come down on one side or another, as he maintains that all things can be true under God and concludes that he would place such stories, however improbable or incredible, 'among those particulars which are neither to be affirmed, nor too positively denied'.. It is interesting to reflect how many stories have followed not dissimilar lines over the years, for example Voltaire's *Candide* and Defoe's *Gulliver's Travels*, to name but two. The moral folk tale continues throughout generations and also plays a major part in Welsh folklore. But believable or not, it was a good tale for a dark March evening.

Chapter 9
Passage over Afon Loughor and the two Gwendraeth streams, and Cydweli

Gerald once again had to cross over water, in this case over two streams and a river, which, must have been quite a strenuous task for the party. We do not know how they crossed these rivers. However, as Gerald mentions in the next chapter that he crossed another river, the Tywi, in a boat, his silence must lead to the conclusion that they were able to ford the Gwendraeth and Loughor without too much difficulty. The estuary of the Loughor is fairly wide and long in depth but it was fordable near to Loughor castle. This castle was on the site of an old a Roman fort and for this reason the old Roman road ran from Neath to Carmarthen through Loughor, and they would have used it accordingly. Gerald does not draw attention to the castle, which stands on a hill on the east bank of the estuary and is now a little away from the main road. The site of a Roman fort stands on a hill commanding the river and also the access by the ford. In the early twelfth century the Normans built a ringwork castle there to extend their control and hold over the area, but in 1151 it was attacked and burnt down by the Welsh, in an effort to reclaim their lands.

By the time Gerald passed by, a new castle had been built by the Normans, who had repaired the structure, adding several stone buildings. The keep, which is still visible, was not added until the next century. The fording of the river was probably uppermost in Gerald's mind.

Following the Roman road they would have passed over the low marshes, which are now the home of the Wetlands and Wild Fowl Trust, passing by what is now the small town of Burry Port. Burry Port's claim to fame is that on 28 June 1928, Amelia Earhart, the first woman to fly the Atlantic, landed there in her seaplane. The thought that people could fly, other than celestial beings, would have seemed a miracle to Gerald.

They next would have passed by Pembrey, where there was a Norman earthwork and a church, dedicated to St Illtud, which was founded in 1066–1075. It has a tower, painted white, overlooking the marshes and the sea. It is an interesting feature that many of the coastal churches are or were painted white externally. This made them clearly visible to the passing sailors as landmarks. Turning to the north they reached Cydweli, where they probably spent the night at the castle.

Cydweli has a fine castle built on a prominent ridge commanding the river Gwendraeth and the surrounding countryside. It was established in about 1106 by King Henry I's minister, Roger, Bishop of Salisbury. Roger was apparently a prodigious builder and, though nothing remains of his original castle, the present ruins are effectively in the form of his original design. One side of the castle is on the edge of an escarpment which drops sharply to the river. On the other side there would have been a semi-circular earthen bank and ditch in the form of a large crescent, giving the castle its present shape. The main buildings and defensive system would have been constructed in timber, leaving it vulnerable to fire. Indeed it fell to Lord Rhys (Rhys ap Gruffudd) to burn it down in 1159. However, it must have been reconstructed by Gerald's visit in 1188, probably again in timber form. It is thought that there may have been a stone hall in the centre of the earthworks, but no evidential remains have been found. It is chronicled that in 1190 Lord Rhys undertook to construct various buildings at Cydweli, although much of the work may only have been reconstruction or repair of the old castle and the new structures would have involved masonry work. The present castle was largely constructed in the thirteenth century, when much of the curtain walls were built together with the inner ward which is defended both by walls and by four formidable towers. The most impressive feature, however, is the fourteenth-century fortified gatehouse which dominates the approaches to the castle. It was the dwelling of the Constable of the castle and it acts as a reminder of the strength and wealth of the lords of Cydweli. The grandeur of the ruins was captured in a fine watercolour by J. M. W. Turner in 1835 (Harris Museum and Art Gallery, Preston) and the splendour of the castle exists to this day. Much of the castle remains and one can imagine it towering above the banks of the Gwendraeth looming out from an early mist.

Gerald recalls that it was in the region of Cydweli that Lord Rhys's wife Gwenllian had led an army against the Normans, while her husband was away seeking reinforcements. She was defeated by Maurice de Londres, the same Maurice who had founded Ewenni Priory. Gwenllian and her two sons were captured and she and one of her sons had their heads cut off, possibly on the battlefield but equally possibly, some historians say, in the castle. This occurred in 1136 and is a reminder of the turbulent times not so many years before Gerald's journey. The site of the battlefield is still called Maes Gwenllian in her memory, and there is a memorial to her nearby.

Gerald also tells a story about Maurice de Londres himself. He owned in the area a forest, which was well stocked with deer and game, about which he was very possessive. His wife, before her sad demise, decided to play a trick on him, knowing him to be very jealous of his possessions and also to be a simple sort of man. She told him that it surprised her that he did not control his animals properly and in particular that his deer seemed to be able to go and do whatever they wished. Indeed, she said, they had been attacking his sheep and the more they killed the poorer the flock, and the less Maurice's wealth became. To prove the story she had two stags killed and their innards filled with wool as evidence. Needless to say Maurice fell for the story and set his hounds out to attack, and one assumes, cull the deer population. It seems a fairly heartless trick to play, particularly bearing in mind the fate of the deer. One assumes that he never found out his wife's trick or had he done so one imagines his humour, being a simple soldier, might have been much strained. Perhaps there is rather more to the story than Gerald relates.

Just below the castle approach there is a plaque inserted in the wall of a small chapel by the Cydweli Civic Society. It relates to the Victorian age and the development of the town and records that a Jacob Chivers (1815–1877) who, as the owner of the local tin works, modernised his plant by introducing steam power to the works and arranged for a piped water supply to be brought to the town. He was not only a philanthropist but was an English-speaker as opposed to a Welsh-speaker. He was borne in Forest of Dean and built the chapel in 1866 so that he and others could worship in the English language. It gives a brief glimpse of the life of the town and the industry and changes which came to this part of Wales in the mid Victorian era. It is surprising to think that from 1737 on the area around Cydweli was the centre of the tinplate industry and that by the end of the nineteenth century was supplying over a half of the world's tinplate requirements.

St Mary's at Cydweli is a large church, crowned with a high stone spire which rises in five stages to dominate the building below. It was originally a Benedictine priory, founded in about 1110, and would thus have been in existence when Gerald passed by. It is just possible that they might have passed the night with the monks rather than at the castle.

Chapter 10
The river Tywi, Carmarthen, and the monastery of Whitland

Yet another river looms in front of the party, but this time Gerald clearly states that they crossed over the Tywi by boat. On the journey to Whitland, three other rivers would also have to be crossed, the Taff, the Cleddau and a tributary of the Cleddau at Haverfordwest. Up above Cydweli the road passes Llansaint where there is a church which dates back to Gerald's time and which he no doubt would have passed. It is now dominated by a high tower, painted white, which was added in the fourteenth century, and overlooks the entire local coastline, acting as a watchtower as well as a landmark. On crossing the Tywi, presumably at the village of Ferryside, Gerald mentions that they left the two castles of Llansteffan and Laugharne, which are clearly visible on the north side of the estuary on the rocks away to the left.

It has been suggested that rather than just crossing the estuary they sailed northwards up the estuary, which would have made more sense than riding up the south side of the estuary.

Both Llansteffan and Laugharne castles are still very evident and are clear signs of Norman power. In the further distant Laugharne castle Rhys ap Gruffudd met with King Henry II where they reached some form of accord or peace in 1171–72. However, immediately after the king's death in 1189, and in an effort to reclaim his lands, Rhys raised enough support locally to be able to take both Laugharne and Llansteffan, although he was unable to take the bigger Carmarthen castle. This is a mere year after Gerald passed by, and emphasises how quickly the political landscape changed in the twelfth century. Nevertheless, we must remember that Gerald and the party were the guests of Rhys during their journey through his territory and were well looked after throughout by him. It will be recalled that Rhys had met with Gerald and Baldwin at Radnor, initially greeting them there some fifteen days earlier. However, there were some straws in the wind which might have indicated that all was not completely as peaceable as it seemed. After their initial meeting Rhys returned home to prepare to go on the Crusade but was talked out of it by his wife Gwenllian, who exerted her persuasive womanly wiles and charms on Rhys so he became uncommitted.

Rhys had been approached by several of the canons of St David, who had strongly urged him not to allow the visitation of the Archbishop of Canterbury to proceed through his lands. They tried to make the case that Baldwin's journey around Wales would seriously damage the prestige of the see of St David's, and that thereby Rhys's own prestige and that of Wales would be diminished. However, 'Although these pleas were most strenuously urged, the natural kindness and civility of the Prince would not suffer them to prevail, lest by prohibiting the Archbishop's progress he might appear to wound his feelings.' Rhys allowed the journey to continue. Gerald's words tell us of the power of Rhys but despite his 'natural kindness' he was also a ruthless man of war. It is probable that Gerald, a relative of Rhys, used his diplomatic skills and influence in arranging the tour through Rhys's lands, despite the fact that it might not have been in Gerald's best interests to do so, as his own ambition was to see the church of Wales separated from the oversight of Canterbury! He no doubt felt he was playing a long-term political game.

A little distance from Carmarthen up the Tywi valley is a folly which Gerald would have enjoyed, had he seen it, because of its bizarreness. This is a three-story tower, known as Paxton's tower which stands on the top of a high hill. It has the most fantastic views for miles around, with the Tywi valley one one side and Carmarthenshire on the other. The deviation from the route is worth it for the view itself. The Victorian folly was built by Sir William Paxton in honour of Admiral Lord Nelson, and its location is such that it can be seen from a long way off. It is triangular with three supporting towers in which there are areas for food preparation, as its use was also as a picnic spot. The carriages would drive under the tower and the guests would climb to the top of the tower to a flat area for their picnics and the spectacular views. It was a picnic with attitude (and altitude)!

Gerald and Baldwin reached the town of Carmarthen on Sunday 20 March. Carmarthen had been built on the site of a Roman camp and fort. This was an important strongpoint over the ages as many main roads met there and travellers required the protection of the town and its inhabitants. Gerald tells us that the city was enclosed by brick walls which were still standing from Roman times. The party probably stayed the night at Carmarthen. Gerald relates that Carmarthen means the 'town of Merlin' as myth had it that Merlin flourished there about the year 450 and had been discovered there, according to ancient sources, as 'the offspring of an incubus'. The town was surrounded by woods and meadowlands and the nearby forests inland from Carmarthen offered a safe refuge for many in those days, though not Rhys ap Gruffudd, who was more by stratagem than by force compelled to surrender there, in 1163, to Henry II, and was carried away to England. Subsequently, Gerald relates, Henry sent one of his knights with the dean of Cantref Mawr, who was clearly a supporter of Rhys, to inspect and report back on the strength and defences of

Dinefwr castle, which was then Rhys's stronghold. The dean was asked to show the knight the easiest and most pleasant route, but instead he took him through the most difficult and inaccessible terrain. Also when they came to a clearing the dean ate a handful of grass to give the impression that the locals were able to survive on grass and roots. The knight reported back that the land was quite uninhabitable and not worth the effort of conquest, there being no roads, and that the inhabitants were bestial and behaved like animals. Henry, on the assumption that Dinefwr and the area was of no interest to him, made Rhys swear his fealty by an oath of allegiance and giving of hostages, and then sent him from England back to Wales.

As seen from the approach from the south, Carmarthen is still dominated by the remains of the Norman castle and city walls, built in 1105, which now surround the muncipal offices and car park. One can still go to one of the remaining towers from which one can look over the river and see how strong the fortifications must have been in the middle ages, and how its prominence had reinforced the administrative importance of Carmarthen to the Normans, as it had been to the Romans before them.

Gerald tells us that after they had left Carmarthen, and as they were making their way towards Whitland abbey, Archbishop Baldwin was told of how a young Welshman, obviously determined to be signed with the cross, had been murdered by his enemies. Baldwin turned aside and ordered the bloody corpse of the young man to be wrapped in a cloak and commended his soul to heaven. The next day twelve archers from the castle at St Clears, which is a little over two thirds of the distance to Whitland from Carmarthen, who were responsible for the murder of the young man, were signed with the cross at Whitland as punishment for their crime. It is interesting that being signed was regarded as a punishment for, as we have seen earlier, it was more importantly regarded as an honour, both spiritually as well as, hopefully, financially to go on the Crusades. One wonders how the twelve archers would have felt about their conscription, but they probably regarded themselves lucky to escape with their lives, as did the released prisoners at Usk. Despite their lives being spared, for the short term at least, their forcible recruitment would still not have been very good news. as they were not knights or of the higher echelon of the aristocracy.

The party would have passed by St Clears, which stands between the rivers Taff and Cynin, on their way. The castle Gerald mentions was a small motte-and-bailey building, which was then at the top end of the navigable part of the river, and it is still highly visible near the present town. There was also a small Cluniac foundation dating from about 1100. More recently two characters are associated with St Clears. The first, the most infamous, was a Mr. Baines, who is reputed as being the last man in Britain to be hung for the crime of forging bank notes. This was in the 1860s. More recently and far more importantly Dylan Thomas (1914–1953) lived in nearby Laugharne.

They finally arrived at what must have been a very fine and well-endowed abbey at Whitland and were no doubt well entertained there for the night. Whitland was founded by the white monks of the Cistercian order and established in 1151. It expanded greatly and at one time it may have housed up to 100 monks and so was a large establishment. The house appears to have ended on the wrong side of the political divide, as it was looted by the English in 1285 and was further damaged in 1294/5. Its deterioration, partially through these problems but also because of the Black Death, meant that by 1440 there were only eight monks in residence. The dissolution under Henry VIII finally ensured its demise and it was effectually razed to the ground.

One can still see part of the old walls and pillars just above ground level. With some imagination one can see how the abbey would have been a bustling and thriving community in Gerald's time in a peaceful and very rural setting. A ground plan sets out in detail the numerous buildings supporting the abbey as well as the religious buildings themselves were laid out.

As has been mentioned, in the morning, the party had to cross three more rivers, the Taff, the Cleddau near to Llawhaden, and another branch of the Cleddau. Whilst they passed Llawhaden to move on to Haverfordwest for the night they could easily have stayed the night at Llawhaden castle, which was one of the several major residences of the Bishop of St David's. The bishop must have been extremely wealthy, and it is recorded that, even in the eighth century, Llawhaden was one of seven bishop's houses in what was then Dyfed. The bishops were powerful, both temporally and spiritually, and moved round touring their estates to ensure that their wealth, or rather that of the church, was well tended and their power maintained. It is recorded that Gerald visited his uncle Bishop David Fitzgerald (1148–1176) in 1175 at Llawhaden.

The present remains of the castle or palace date from the reign of Bishop Adam de Houghton (1362–1389), who built new suites and apartments increasing the Palace first founded by Bishop Bernard in 1115.

There is also an interesting church, which dates back to before the Normans, at Llawhaden, dedicated to St Aidan. It has a large square tower with another slightly smaller tower attached to it giving a further defence from a double tower, which is a very unusual combination. The entrance to the church is guarded by four yew trees which give the churchyard a very atmospheric feeling, and indicates that the church and its site go back to pre-Norman times.

In the twelfth century this would have been a stone church and it is possible that Gerald stopped there and preached by the outdoor cross as he passed by, although he gives no mention of this. In a recess against the south wall of the church is a stone figure of a tonsured priest and legend has it that this is St Hugo or even St Aidan, but there is no confirmation that this is so. There are several features of interest in the church, including a twelfth-century font, a memorial to Evan Owen who was chaplain to King Charles II and Chancellor of St David's, and several strange roundels.

Chapter 11
Haverfordwest and Rhos

Haverfordwest was the site of much preaching. Archbishop Baldwin delivered his sermon which was followed by another from Gerald which he, in his typically modest way, tells us was preached with great eloquence. Indeed so eloquent was his sermon that even though he preached in both Latin and French – notably neither in Welsh nor English – the large crowd of both civilians and soldiers, who would not have understood a word, were (according to Gerald!) so moved by Gerald's words that they gave vent to as much emotion and tears as those who did understand, and were so overcome that they rushed forward to receive the sign of the cross quickly and with much enthusiasm. Such enthusiasm compares strangely with the reaction to 'punishment' administered to the twelve archers of St Clears. However, the rush of emotion was an occurrence which even Gerald found odd, and thought it, in a self-effacing way, even miraculous. Certainly the way Gerald relates the incident it would seem that Baldwin's sermon must have been somewhat work-a-day and that he was eclipsed by the Archdeacon of St David's' powerful rendition.

However, he does allow the Archbishop to regain the high moral ground by describing a miracle brought on through Baldwin's spiritual power. An old woman who had been blind for three years sent her son to hear the sermons and, in particular, to bring back something tangible from the Archbishop, even if it was only a thread of his clothing. The crowds were so great that he could not get near to Baldwin, but after all the crowds had dispersed he dug up a piece of the turf on which Baldwin had been standing when giving the sign of the cross, and took it back to his mother. She was delighted and knelt in prayer pressing the turf to her mouth and eyes. Needless to say, thanks to the power of Baldwin's spirit and her own faith she immediately recovered the sight which she had previously lost completely. So in miraculous terms Gerald and Baldwin came out with honours equal in spirituality at Haverfordwest. But despite the miracle Baldwin was never canonised.

Many of the people of Haverfordwest were evacuees from Flanders who had effectively colonised the area, and had not integrated themselves with the local people. Despite being brave and robust, they were in constant conflict with the locals. The Welsh Chronicler wrote that in:

> The yeare of 1108, the rage of the sea did overflow, and drownd a great part of the lowe countrie of Flanders, insuch that the inhabitants were driven to seek themselves other dwelling places, who came to King Henry and desired him to give them some void place to remaine in, who being very liberal of that which was not his owne, gave them the land of Ros, on Dyrel or West Wales, where Pembroke, Tenby and Haverford are now built, and there they remaine to this daie, as may well be perceived by ther speech and conditions, farre differing from the rest of the countrie.

They were skilled in the wool trade but were also capable of working hard on the land or as soldiers, but Gerald laments that if only Wales could have a better place in the hearts of its rulers, or if those in power locally would not deal so harshly and stop ill-treating Welsh people, co-existence would be much improved.

Gerald relates that the Flemings also had the power of

divination and could apply this by reading the right shoulder-blades of rams. To use their power it was necessary for them to boil the meat off the bone and then, by inspecting carefully the indentations, lumps and markings on the bone, they were able to determine when there would be peace or war, fires or murder, infidelities of married people and the life and death of kings. Gerald exemplifies this by relating to an event in his own time concerning a William Mangunel. William had some knowledge of divination and his wife had the power as a diviner. His wife had been made pregnant by William's grandson, which to us seems well nigh unbelievable, but given the age of marriage and puberty in Gerald's time it is feasible. William was aware of the circumstances and took a ram from his own flock and gave it to his wife to prepare, she thinking it was a present from a neighbour. At dinner that evening, the ram having been cooked according to the correct ritual, William passed the shoulder-blade to his wife for her divination which he knew would be accurate. She inspected the bone and then with a smile threw it on the table. William asked her what she had read from the bone and the reason for her laughter to which she responded that the man from whose flock the ram had come has a wife who had broken her marriage vows and had intercourse and is pregnant by his grandson. William, with a gloomy face, said that she spoke the truth and that the facts supported her results and that he would have to bear the disgrace of her infidelity and of being cuckolded. His wife tried to cover up her confusion; her face went bright pink and then pale and, as Gerald states, 'lastly (according to the custom of women) by tears'. However, Gerald does not relate how the two of them resolved the issue; this must be left to the reader's imagination.

He tells further stories about the use of these bones. In one case the bone of a goat was used as opposed to a ram, and the diviner told the person seeking his message that his herd would not increase in number. It never did. Many diviners foretold the devastation which would hit Wales after Henry I died, even up to some year and a half before the event itself. Based on this advice they sold up all their property and thus avoided financial disaster. This might be a useful tool for use in prophesying periods of financial instability and crisis.

In Gerald's time another teller of bones predicted not only a theft, but also established the perpetrator, time and place of the event and also stated that simultaneously he could hear both bells ringing and a trumpet sounding. All of which happened: so prognostications of both sound, events and those guilty could be made at the same time.

Even in the early 1800s Hoare tells us that the young women of Rhos still consulted a ram's shoulder-blade to see whom they should marry. Earlier in Chaucer's Canterbury Tales the parson condemns 'thilke horrible swering of adjuracioun and conjuracioun ... in a shulder-boon of a sheep'. And the practice even occurred as far away as China as 'Two ox scapulae treated for oracle-taking, excavated at Anyang, Honan,' were exhibited in a Chinese Archaeological Exhibition held in London in 1973–1974. Also ram's shoulder-blades were used in Tartar magic rituals, as well as many Turkish-speaking nomadic tribes, and rams' shoulder-blades were used as sacred objects in some ceremonies. So shoulder-bones should not be lightly cast away, but should be properly used.

So, from shoulder-blades we turn back to Haverfordwest. The town was built where there was the lowest ford through the Cleddau and the Old Bridge, built in 1726, now stands at that point. It was this ford which Henry, Earl of Richmond (Tudor) crossed in 1485 having landed near Milford Haven on his way to the Battle of

Bosworth and eventual kingship. Gerald and his party would have availed themselves of the same ford some three hundred years earlier. They may have stayed at the castle, which stands on a high naturally defended ridge with a sheer cliff to the east.

It was established originally by Tancard or Tankred, one of the Flemish immigrants, in the form of a motte-and-bailey, but this was further developed by Gilbert de Clare, Earl of Pembroke, who started building the stone castle soon after 1135. Henry II stayed at what must have been a substantial building in 1173 and Gerald and Baldwin arrived a mere fifteen years later. The castle was further developed in the 1200s by William Marshal, Earl of Pembroke. More particularly much of the presently existing fabric was due to Eleanor of Acquitaine, who on her way to St David's on a Royal Pilgrimage with Edward I must have taken a fancy to the castle. She bought it in 1289 and spent a considerable sum on improvements to the buildings for her own use. Over the years since the castle was constructed it served as a prison but, specifically in 1797, the prison which had been built in 1779 in the inner ward was used to incarcerate 415 French prisoners from an abortive French invasion, and further Frenchmen were held there after the Spanish Peninsular War.

The old Governor's house still stands from that time and now contains the Town Museum. Nearby there is a substantial 'new' prison building built in 1820. In the outer ward the County Records Office is currently housed, so the site has remained in constant use over many years up to the present day.

It is possible that Gerald's earth-shaking sermon was preached near or at St Mary's church, which stands a little distant from the castle up a steep incline. Most of St Mary's dates from the thirteenth century with many subsequent additions and alterations and nothing appears to remain from Norman times. The lack of any remnant may be because the town was burnt by Llywelyn the Great in 1220 and the original church would have been seriously damaged, if not destroyed. There are several examples of carving from the thirteenth century. Two are thought to have been carved to mock Welsh culture, one being of a pig playing a crwth, an early stringed instrument. The second was of an ape playing a harp. There is even a carving of a man with a toothache left to suffer in posterity. There is a special wooden pew which is for the use of the Mayor or Sheriff of Haverfordwest. It has a rich carving of St Michael slaying the dragon surmounted with the arms of France and England and a poppy head which are said to date it to about 1415 and the time of Agincourt. Poppies were a reminder of war even in the 1400s.

Gerald and the retinue probably stayed the two nights of 22 and 23 March at the castle, particularly as it had already served as a royal residence and must have been reasonably comfortable. He tells in some detail of an incident at the castle. A notorious prisoner was being held in chains and three boys, one the son of the Earl of Clare, used to visit the prisoner regularly, in particular to get arrows, as he was very adept at fitting iron heads to the arrows for their use. On one occasion they asked that the prisoner be allowed out into the fresh air, the usual gaoler being absent. The prisoner seized his chances and slammed the doors to his prison shut, with him and the boys inside, and threatened to kill the boys with an axe he had obtained. In the event his desperate action worked and he was promised his life and given every surety he required. So he released the boys and spent a life of freedom thereafter. It is thought that one of the boys was the castellan's son Robert, the castellan being Richard FitzTancard, son of the original builder of the castle. Gerald also tells a similar story concerning the chateau of Chateauroux in France which ended in a rather different way. In this case the prisoner who had abducted the castellan's son rather than achieving his freedom leapt over the castle walls carrying and killing his hostage in revenge for his ill-treatment. Both died at what was called the Scene of Sorrows.

Chapter 12
Pembrokeshire

Gerald now effectively halts his journey to talk about the neighbouring province of Rhos, namely Pembroke. This is very much the place of his earlier life as he was born and brought up in the province, and he is obviously more than happy to describe his county with great affection. One can almost hear him telling his fellow travellers during the stay in Haverfordwest all about his home and memories.

He refers to Pembroke itself, the capital of Dyfed in those times, as built high on a rock above the sea. Gerald suggests that the Welsh name, *Penfro*, means 'head of the estuary', but it is better translated as 'head of the end of a region', or even 'land's end'. It is now dominated by the impressive ruins of Pembroke castle, which protected the town and the route to Ireland. The original castle was built by Arnulf de Montgomery in about 1091, being made of 'wooden staves and turf', but nevertheless it was a very strong fort. Arnulf left the fortress, going to England, and appointed Gerald of Windsor, Gerald's grandfather, as his Castellan. The castle was put under siege and Gerald, being 'a worthy and discreet man', used an interesting stratagem to lift the siege. Just as the garrison was on its last legs he took four hogs, which was pretty well all the besieged had left for food, cut them into sections and hurled them over the fortifications at his besiegers to show them that they had plenty of food in the castle and could sustain their defence for a long time to come. He also wrote a letter, making sure it would be intercepted, to the then Bishop of St David's, Wilfred, who was by chance in that neighbourhood, presumably at his palace at Lamphey, saying that the fortress would have no need for provisions or reinforcements for at least four months. The Welsh, on hearing this, believed that it was going to be a long time before they could take Pembroke, abandoned the siege, and went home, as it was not worth going to all the hassle of a long siege. Boredom played a great part in the wars of the day!

A William Marshall in 1189, one year after our journey, unhorsed King Henry II's rebellious son Richard (later King Richard the Lionheart) in a skirmish and spared his life. In recompense Richard rewarded him with the hand of the daughter of Richard de Clare who was heiress to significant estates in Wales and Ireland and Marshall prospered greatly as 'king' of the Marches. It is always a good idea to spare a king's son!

The palace of Lamphey is one of the many the Bishop of St David's inhabited, including his magnificent palace at St David's where Gerald was to arrive shortly. The palace at Llawhaden has already been discussed. Gerald's reference to the palace at Lamphey is the first reference to it as a bishop's palace. Sadly there are no remains of what would have been a series of timber buildings, which would, no doubt, have been of excellent construction, wealth and quality. The earliest remains now seen probably date from the thirteenth century. Nevertheless the palace must have been pretty substantial, as Gerald was to upbraid Bishop Geoffrey de Henlaw in 1210–12 for staying with all his retinue at other places nearby rather than using his own palace at Lamphey. No doubt the bishop was cutting costs!

The present buildings in the main date from the work carried out by Bishop Henry de Gower (1328–1347) who was also mainly responsible for the building of the Bishop's palace at St David's. The shell of his great hall at Lamphey measures some 25 metres long and arcaded parapets are used as decoration similar to the style of the parapets which can be seen at St David's.

The Black Book of St David's recorded that in 1326, even before de Gower's works, there were stone houses within the walls and outside, two water mills, a windmill, four fishponds and a considerable area of parkland. There was also a considerable range of feudal duties and agricultural services owed to the bishop, so overall his wealth in the 1300s was huge, and even though Gerald's time was a hundred years earlier, the wealth of the bishopric must have been as substantial. The spiritual as well as the temporal powers of the bishop must have been significant particularly as St David's was a centre of pilgrimage. Two pilgrimages to St David's were worth the equivalent of one to Jerusalem in view of the difficulties of terrain and the wildness of the land, and the endowments from such pilgrimages by royal and wealthy patrons would be considerable, as would the proceeds from the sale of indulgences and religious artefacts. The benefit of a pilgrimage was to allow the pilgrim commutation of some of his time in Purgatory and thus entry into heaven at a quicker rate than normal. The purchase of indulgences also speeded things along!

St David's being on the route to Ireland would have further increased its wealth. The remains and extent of Lamphey alone speak of the episcopal powers and wealth, with its three large halls, residences, storage cellars, produce barns, gatehouses and defences. When one adds in the rest of the properties and rents owed to the bishop it is difficult to contemplate in modern days how extremely rich the church in Gerald's day was. To be a bishop in the 1300s was a career beyond imagination.

Whilst Gerald does not tell us any detail about Lamphey he does tell us that about three miles from Pembroke is a fortified mansion called Manorbier, which was where Gerald's family came from and where he was borne. He asks forgiveness for lavishing praise on his home, but it was his home! His words set out vividly his love, memories and visions of Manorbier:

> It is excellently well defended by turrets and bulwarks, and is situated on the summit of a hill extending on the western side towards the sea-port, having on the northern and southern sides a fine fish-pond under its walls, as conspicuous for its grand appearance, as for the depth of its waters, and a beautiful orchard on the same side, inclosed on one part by a vineyard, and on the other by a wood, remarkable for the projection of its rocks, and the height of its hazel trees. On the right hand of the promontory, between the castle and the church, near the site of a very large lake and mill, a rivulet of never-failing water flows through a valley, rendered sandy by the violence of the winds . . . This country is well supplied with corn, sea-fish and imported wines; and what is preferable to every other advantage, from its vicinity to Ireland, is tempered by a salubrious air . . . It is evident, therefore, that Maenor Pirr [Manorbier] is the pleasantest spot in Wales; and the author may be pardoned for having thus extolled his native soil, his genial territory, with a profusion of praise and adoration.

This is praise indeed.

To the observant and imaginative tourist standing in Manorbier, Gerald's words are as appropriate today as they were to him. The fishpond has gone but the hazelnut trees remain. The view down to the sea and beach are the same but perhaps the sea and shoreline is a little further away from Manorbier than Gerald would remember.

The stream winds down to the sea, although it is difficult to envisage the harbour until one remembers that the ships of those days were so small as to be able to make what appears now to be a small stretch of navigable water. The sea would have been higher and closer to the castle in his day. The church is there across the valley and the fortified mansion which William de Barri constructed and lived in, possibly erected by the Flemish, is largely the building one now sees. William and his wife Angharad de Barri were Gerald's parents and he was their youngest son. Without being too romantic one can almost feel the presence of Gerald walking through the old halls and the passages around Manorbier, looking down towards the sea, watching the boats from Ireland being propelled by the winds at the end of the bay. One can imagine him when young playing within the courtyard, or in the fields and orchards outside the walls and even, if they did so in his time, making sandcastles on the beach! It is, despite Gerald's hyperbole, a very special place.

The buildings have survived in reasonable order as they escaped any military problems or incursions. Perhaps this survival from the administration of Lord Rhys, who ravaged the area but seems to have by-passed Manorbier, is due to his family ties which encouraged him to leave his relatives unmolested. Even so Manorbier was a fortified mansion, rather than a full-blown castle as Gerald states; but it was well guarded. It was not without problems, however: in 1153 Gerald, a young boy of seven, sought refuge across the valley in the parish church, rather than remain in the house during a fierce attack by Rhys ap Gruffudd on nearby Tenby against Norman domination. Even in 1187, the year before Gerald's journey, Maelgwyn ap Rhys led an army of Welshmen into Tenby. In the event, Gerald's security was assured.

The church one sees today is just across the valley and is dominated by a white tower but it was built a little later than when Gerald sought refuge, in about 1250. The chancel was also rebuilt about that time, probably on an existing foundation. It is a 'weeping chapel'. In the north end of the transept is an effigy of a knight carrying the de Barri arms. This could be John de Barri (1324), although a notice now states that it is probably of Walter de Barri, Gerald's half-brother.

Gerald does not mention any other specific places in Pembrokeshire but the county has many historical buildings and memorials. The Carew cross dates back to the early years of the eleventh century and bears comparison with the cross at Nevern, which we will see as Gerald continues on his way to north Wales. Carew castle, which dates back to before the Normans, is a magnificent castle with many Elizabethan connections, not least that its owner Sir John Perrot was sentenced to death for treason in 1592. In the event he died in the Tower of London from natural causes. There are other Elizabethan connections with Lamphey palace, which itself was the home of Robert Devereux, second earl of Essex, and favourite of Queen Elizabeth I. He was not as lucky as Sir John Perrot, as he was beheaded in the Tower. The Earl of Leicester, another of Elizabeth's favourites, is said to have been given by the Queen the great house at Laleston, as a hunting lodge. It is alleged that he had several liaisons with the local ladies at the lodge! But all this was centuries after Gerald's time. Gerald does, however, relate many strange local happenings in Pembroke and elsewhere that we shall touch on in brief.

These allegedly contemporary happenings concern unclean spirits and their activities. The first story concerns an apparition in the house of a Stephen Wiriet and then William Not, and seem to have been what we would know as the presence in the form of a poltergeist. Not only was the apparition given to throwing refuse all over the place but also to ripping up the clothing of the owners of the houses and their guests. In Stephen's house the spirits, even though they could not be seen, would argue with people, remonstrating about all the nasty acts they, the guests, had done in their lifetime that had been better kept secret. Gerald is unable to explain the manifestations except to say they often happen when the victims have changed their circumstances from poverty to wealth or vice versa. Also he is bemused as the clergy were unable to cleanse or cast out the spirits as they were accustomed to do, but had filth thrown over them too. Rather plaintively he comments that the sacraments seemingly are no use against such trifling matters as poltergeists but only against real harm, and they are of no use against the use of one's own imagination! He draws an analogy with a woman from Poitou who was possessed of the devil, against whom the use of relics or the Bible was ineffective. The devil stated that the reason he was not exorcised was that he only had power over the woman's body and not over her soul. He was safe as all the remedies including the sacraments were only to rid him from the soul and not the body of his victim. A nice distinction which could not have given much comfort to the woman possessed.

An Elidyr of Stackpole had to deal with a full incarnation of a spirit in the form of a red headed man called Simon. This Simon acted as a perfect servant, never sleeping in the house but he was always punctual and reliable. He was dismissed from service, despite his dependability, after he was seen talking with fellow demons next to a nearby watermill. He turned out to be the son of a mad lady and, allegedly, had been fathered by an incubus – and the widow, who was still alive, confirmed the story! It was rather hard on Simon who had worked hard for at least forty days for Elidyr. A similar occurrence happened to an archbishop in

Denmark. A priest attached himself to the clergyman and, after telling him that he was a devil, vanished without trace. The church could be infiltrated by evil spirits, as well as the laity. In this vein Gerald is also concerned how lightning often strikes churches and destroys religious artefacts but that God does nothing to stop such desecration. He quotes Peter Abelard as stating that lightning always strikes the loftier things in life but never a public lavatory!

Lightning could be even more selective, as was seen in a dispute in France between some Cistercian monks and a knight who owned land which the Cistercians believed was theirs. In a violent storm all the Cistercian crops were destroyed, but none of the knight's. He claimed that God had arbitrated on his side so the land was really his. The abbot continued the dispute as he considered that the storm was the work of the devil who was, they assumed, naturally friendly to the knight as he did not have holy orders. In their view the devil only showed hostility to the holy and righteous monks. The result of the arbitration is not recorded but no doubt the church triumphed in the end.

Finally he comments that the falcons which were bred in the region were exceptionally good hunting birds, and that Henry II when staying in the region in 1171 saw the effectiveness of the birds. Henry subsequently always sent to Pembroke to obtain some at breeding time as he could not find any hounds so good for hunting in his entire kingdom. After all these stories and information about Pembroke Gerald states, 'But let us return to our Itinerary'.

Chapter 13
Camrose and Newgale to St David's

After their rest at Haverfordwest Gerald and Baldwin set out for St David's, the highlight of their journey, a distance of about twelve miles. It is the first time Gerald has mentioned distances. They were to pass through Camrose and then across Newgale Sands before reaching their objective, and a well-earned rest of probably three days, before turning north up the coast. This followed an old road slightly to the north of the present main road, meeting up with the new road at Roch.

Camrose had, at that time, a small but strong motte-and-bailey castle guarding a small ford. It had been established around 1080 and it is reputed that William the Conqueror stayed in the castle on his way to St David's on pilgrimage. The site is now completely overgrown but the mound rises to the height of the original motte and there are remains of a small stone wall around the base. The motte itself is a good example of the castles Gerald would have seen on his route, as well as the more developed stone castles. At Roch there is an interesting castle which is now a private residence. It was built originally in the thirteenth century by Adam de la Roche. He was told by a witch that he would be killed one day by a snake, but if he could pass a year in safety then he need never fear vipers. So the castle was built to be safe from snakes. He, in the meantime, went to live in the top of the tower so that he could be completely free from snakes for the year. However, on the very last night of his self-incarceration he was very cold and was sent a basket of wood to allow him to be warm and comfortable but, as he was putting the logs on the fire, an adder crawled out of the basket and bit him. Next day he was found dead.

From Roch Gerald followed the route down to a large and attractive expanse of beach called Newgale Sands. The Sands had a particular association with Tancard, who we have already met at Haverfordwest. Tancard tried to keep the body of St Caradog, who died in 1124, at Haverfordwest, rather than comply with St Caradog's wishes that he be buried at St David's cathedral. Tancard fell ill three times and this concentrated his mind severely as he was conscious of the religious significance of a triple hit! The Pharaoh had to endure three plagues before allowing Moses to depart and Peter denied Jesus three times when he was under questioning. So Tancard gave in to the saint's last wishes. In some ways the analogy between Tancard and the Pharaoh is the greater, as when he let the body go a very severe rainstorm hit those carrying the body across the Sands. Was this another sign of God's wrath? When the carriers emerged sodden from such shelter as they could come across they found that the bier and its silken cover were completely dry. The body was buried in St David's and the tomb is still to be seen under the tower arch at the south side of the north transept in the cathedral. It is thought St Caradog's relics still remain in the tomb. Gerald tells us that the tomb was the cause subsequently of many miracles and he hoped that these miracles would long continue. He also proposed to Pope Innocent III that Caradog be canonised.

In the winter of 1171–1172 there was a huge storm. The force of it was such that the shores of south Wales, including Newgale Sands, were washed away, revealing at Newgale a forest which had been beneath the sand for centuries. Gerald describes the scene graphically, in such a way that he may even have seen the phenomenon himself. 'The surface of the earth, which had been covered for many ages, re-appeared, and discovered [sic] the trunks of trees cut off, standing in the very sea itself, the strokes of the hatchet appearing as if only made yesterday; the soil was very black and the wood like ebony.' Also fish and eels were washed ashore for the local inhabitants to collect. The storm must have been very severe for the petrified forest to have been appeared. Just such a petrified forest can be seen off the shore at Borth, near Aberystwyth, whenever there is an unusually low tide, and must be very similar to that which Gerald witnessed. It is extraordinary that such forests still remain preserved under the sea for such a length of time. But it is not only in salt water that trees are preserved: a forest over 500 years old was discovered in 2005 in the fresh waters of Loch Tay in Scotland.

Gerald's party must have ridden along the sands coming down a steep descent from the surrounding hills on tired horses, to be revived by the salty air and the fact that they had, after three weeks travel, nearly reached their goal. So, after all the journeying, preaching and signing people to the cross the party finally reached St David's where, we are told, they were given good accommodation by Peter de Leia, the Bishop of St David's, who Gerald calls 'a liberal man, who had hitherto accompanied us during the whole of our journey'. One wonders whether Gerald is being a little ironic in his kind description of de Leia, partly as he was foiled in his attempt to become the Bishop of St David's in 1176 by Peter de Leia. In all his journey so far Gerald had only mentioned Peter de Leia once, even though he had shared the trials and tribulations of the whole journey. The one mention is at Radnor, where he followed Gerald's example and took the cross. Gerald was no doubt in a truly forgiving mood, as his disappointment at not being appointed Bishop of St David's had occurred some twelve years earlier. Equally Gerald had not given up on his hopes to be appointed Bishop of St David's, and he still hoped to attain his own ambition of being appointed Archbishop of Wales one day, independent of deferment to Canterbury.

Chapter 14
St David's

It must have been with great relief and not a little excitement when Gerald and the party arrived at St David's on 25 March, and saw spread before them, below the fortified gateway, the cathedral within its protective walls.

The present sight which one now sees has changed considerably from Gerald's day, not least with the building of the 'new palace', but nevertheless it must have been a magnificent vista and a potential oasis of calm and contemplation. St David's was revered as a place of pilgrimage and this would have added to the sense of achievement of having reached halfway in their journey and difficult mission. Most of all St David's must have been for Gerald his spiritual home and the centre of his ambitions (which were, sadly, never to be achieved). There must also have been a little worry in Gerald's mind as to the way in which the Canons of St David's would greet the Archbishop and the form of their hospitality, as they had not wanted Baldwin to visit St David's in the first place. Peter de Leia, the Bishop of St David's, obviously ensured that all were made comfortable.

St David's cathedral shows clearly through its structure the wealth and power of its incumbents. However even more this is shown by the remains of the Bishop Gower's palace dating from the 1330s.

St David's cathedral was a refuge to many pilgrims, including William the Conqueror in 1081. Henry II was twice the guest of Gerald's uncle David Fitzgerald at the bishop's palace which preceded that of Bishop Gower. It is thought that this was an earth and timber castle constructed at Castle Penlan some half a mile from the remains of the new bishop's palace. The first time Henry II dined was in 1171. This was in the bishop's court when he came to attend a mass at the cathedral. He also dined in 1172 at a location unknown but it must have been at the bishop's castle. The earlier castle or palace would have been a very significant dwelling in its own right. Gerald also tells us that Peter de Leia gave them good accommodation, which one assumes was in the old palace or its surrounds. Sadly there are no remains of the earlier palace of Gerald's uncle. Its splendour must have been consistent with the quality of the visitors received there and compatible with the grandeur of the cathedral. It was supported, as we have seen, by very significant proceeds from tithes, endowments and land and from the revenues of those who were travelling on to Ireland.

Gerald gives a report, presumably as an eyewitness, of Henry II's visit on his way back from Ireland. He landed at Porth Stinian, the port of St David's, on Easter Monday 1172. In Gerald's words:

> habited like a pilgrim, and leaning on a staff, he met at the white gate a procession of the canons of the church coming forth to receive him with due honour and reverence. As the procession solemnly moved along, a Welsh woman threw herself at the king's feet, and made a complaint against the bishop of the place.

The bishop was, of course, Gerald's uncle! It was obviously quite a noisy occasion and not befitting the return of the king. As part of her tirade the Welsh woman shouted out a prophecy made by Merlin that a king of England, who had just conquered Ireland, would be wounded in that country by a man with a red hand, and then, on his return to St David's would die as he walked over Llech-lafar – the 'speaking stone' – that served as a bridge over the Afon Alun, the stream which marks the boundary of the cemetery on the north side of the cathedral. The stone was made of very beautiful marble, 'polished by the feet of passengers'. It is still there. The king knew of the prophecy and, possibly with some nervousness, strode across the stone. Once he was across he turned and gave his view on the efficacy of the prophecy! One of the crowd shouted out that the prophecy did not apply to Henry because he had not yet conquered Ireland. (Indeed, has anyone?) Henry went into the cathedral to hear Mass and then went on to his castle at Haverfordwest.

Gerald tells us more about Llech-lafar:

> There was an ancient tradition respecting this stone, that at the time a corpse was carried over it, for interment, it broke forth into speech, and by the effort cracked in the middle, which fissure is still visible; and on account of this barbarous and ancient superstition, the corpses are no longer brought over it.

Gerald tells us two other stories. The first was about the Alun, which he regards as a muddy and unproductive stream. It had, nevertheless, been running with wine at the time of Bishop David II. The other tale concerns a nearby spring called Pistidewi, or St David's spout, which runs into the churchyard to the east not only with water but also from time to time with milk. Incidentally Hoare reports that in his day the river produced trout of a most delicious taste but that no longer applies today. Gerald tells us nothing about either the palace or, more importantly, the cathedral itself. This is disappointing on two counts. Firstly the cathedral must have been of a significant size. It was quite similar to the present cathedral, evidenced by the report of Henry's visit. Secondly Gerald himself was involved with Peter de Leia in building the present cathedral, the work on which started in 1182 and is an example of the flowering of the twelfth-century Romanesque style. It would have been helpful to have information from Gerald about the format and task which was undertaken. A modern statue of Gerald, standing in the Holy Trinity Chapel, commemorates his connection with St David's. His involvement in the building followed the absolution of Gerald's vows to go on the Crusade. It was felt he had a more important role than to die in the Holy Land. Even though he had reached France on the way to the Crusades the absolution was granted, on behalf of the Pope, by the Cardinal Legate John of Anagni in 1189. Anagni also absolved Peter de Leia, but Archbishop Baldwin was not so favoured and carried on into the holy land to die at the siege of Acre in 1190.

At the time of Gerald's journey the cathedral was newly dedicated under Bishop Bernard, the first Norman bishop, who Gerald praises for attempting to recover the rites of St David's. On the down side he did not endow the Chapter with sufficient funds, as he gave away the episcopal properties to various Norman Lords, presumably his friends, as Gerald says 'without either advantage or profit, and disposed of others so indiscreetly and improvidently'. Gerald sums up Bernard in a fairly damning epitaph as being 'remarkable for his insufferable pride and ambition', but this may have been tempered by his own thwarted ambitions. Nothing remains of the 1131 church, which was demolished, and much of the new work begun under Gerald and de Leia between 1180 to 1182 survives today in the present structure. This is particularly evident in the six-bay building of the nave, with alternating round and octagonal pillars, each bay having two small pointed arches above, and the remains of the twelfth century windows. The windows were subsequently altered by Bishop Gower (1328–47) in his reconstruction in the fourteenth century. There are many examples of Gower's rebuilding. In particular, the huge stone screen between the presbytery and the nave is a monument to his work and is where his tomb marks his final resting place.

Inside the screen are the remains of interesting medieval paintings depicting an owl being taunted by magpies, the lion of St Mark, and on one of the pillars a Norman knight. In the quire there is a magnificent carved bishop's throne, which was made for Gower, and there are many other architectural examples dating from his time. Bishop Gower's real triumph is the building of the bishop's palace, and this is emphasised by the epitaph on his tomb, which was taken away during the commonwealth period. This stated 'Here lies Henry Gower, constructor of the Palace'. Also it has been claimed that in the southern aisle of the cathedral Gerald's body lies but, whilst there is a tomb stone carving which obviously represents one of the church dignitaries, there is no inscription to justify the claim that it is Gerald himself. He died in 1223, possibly at Hereford, but it would be nice to think that his wish to be buried in St David's was respected, as that would have been a perfect epitaph to his work both in St David's and for Wales. However, the tomb of the Lord Rhys, who died in 1197, is definitely in the new building which he, perhaps, had helped to finance.

In the shrine itself there is a painted casket that holds the relics or bones of St David, St Justinian and possibly St Caradog. The cathedral is a fascinating building full of carvings from various ages, for example the fifteenth-century choir stalls with their surviving misericords, one of which depicts pilgrims being seasick on board ship! The building reflects, through its architecture, the many changes throughout the centuries. The old parts, with their direct connections to Gerald, merge with the changes through the ages and particularly with the alterations wrought by Gilbert Scott, the great Victorian architect which include the superb ceiling of the tower lantern which was recoloured during his restoration. The cathedral survived from innate problems with topography as part was built on an old riverbed and was liable to subsidence. It survived an earthquake in about 1247 and was relatively unscathed by the ravages of the Civil War and by general neglect during the many years of its history. But, as has already been mentioned, the cathedral through its history recalls all those who visited and worshipped there over the years, many of whom are commemorated in its precinct. There are many tombs as testament to the past, including various bishops' tombs, and the tomb of Edmund Tudor, Earl of Richmond (died 1456), the father of King Henry VII. The Chapel of St Thomas à Becket is a reminder that the saint's bones lay in the important cathedral of St David's until they were removed in 1220 and reinterred in Canterbury Cathedal.

Within a short walk from the cathedral one can find St Non's well and chapel above the cliffs looking out to sea. The small chapel is now virtually a ruin and must have been very simple in construction. It is the tradition that St Non, who was St David's mother, gave birth to him at this spot, during a thunderstorm, and that at the spot a well sprang up at the same time. The well is still there and is said to cure infirmities and to have miraculous properties. One wonders if wells were given to miracles because they were obviously clean and clear water unpolluted from the towns and their sewage and problems. One presumes that a course of clean water over several days would have cured some diseases of Gerald's time. The well still is a place of pilgrimage and there is a religious retreat nearby with a fantastic sea view.

So, after probably three days' respite and rest, on or about Monday 29 March, after the Archbishop had celebrated an early Mass at the high altar in St David's cathedral, the journey, this time to the north, began. They were about halfway through their mission, and they had another gruelling twenty-seven days ahead of them.

Chapter 15
Cemais and St Dogmaels monastery

Gerald does not write so fully about the second part of the journey to the north of Wales and then back to the starting point of Hereford. Possibly this is because the population of the west and north Wales was rather less than that of south Wales or, perhaps, the journey was beginning to take its toll, as was the constant companionship of the core party.

After St David's the party split, as the Archbishop, after saying Mass, rushed off to Cardigan, where Lord Rhys was to welcome Baldwin into the region under his direct control. Gerald was left behind, albeit briefly, to preach to the people of St David's, and then was forced to catch up. Gerald does not tell us how his sermon went down, but as he must have preached often at St David's, in his capacity as Archdeacon, no doubt he acquitted himself in his usual competent fashion.

Gerald met up again with Baldwin, probably the following evening, at St Dogmaels abbey, having passed through the *cantref* of Cemais. As was his wont he tells of two stories concerning the *cantref* (a local district under Welsh law). The first is a sad tale concerning a young man from the area, called Longshanks, who was ill and was persecuted by a plague of toads. Gerald says that it was as though the whole toad population had a wish to visit him and, whilst many toads were killed by his friends, they managed to grow again in number, almost as if they bred again as soon as their heads were cut off. More and more appeared and in the end the defenders against the invasion were fully exhausted. To save their friend they cut down a big tree, defoliated it and hoisted the poor ill man in a bag to the top of the tree. Sadly for him the toads climbed up the tree and ate him up so that only a skeleton remained. For once there does not seem to be a moral to this sad story, nor does Longshanks appear to have been religiously misguided, only ill. Gerald merely opines that the judgement of God is sometimes difficult to understand. He tells of another man who was similarly attacked, this time by rats!

He tells of yet another man who lived in the Preseli mountains who learnt in three consecutive dreams that if he were to put his hand under a stone, which stood above a nearby spring, where the stream gushed out beneath it he would find there a golden torque or bracelet. On the third day after his last dream he went off and did what he was bidden but was bitten by a viper and subsequently died. Gerald points out that some times dreams are true, sadly not in this case, but that one must pick and choose which dreams are true and which are not by using common sense. This advice seems, to say the least, to lead to a very random selection of actions based on dreams. For what must be assumed to have been a relatively poor man one assumes that he possibly did use his common sense and hopes; regrettably there were dire consequences.

The route taken by the party must have been along the flattish land above the cliffs rather than along the shore, and it would have passed by what is now Fishguard (*Abergwaun*). The origins of the name 'Fishguard' may have stemmed from the Scandinavians as it derives from a Norse word meaning a 'fish catching enclosure'; the Welsh name means 'at the mouth of the river Gwaun'. Although there is no historic evidence for a Scandinavian settlement, there is evidence of a Norman one which lay along what is now the High Street and there are some remains of a motte at its south end. Fishguard may therefore have been a small hamlet in Gerald's time. It now is a pleasant town with a pretty harbour. Its main claim to history is that it was the site of the last invasion of Britain in 1797, this time by some fourteen hundred French in four warships. Their initial plan had been to land near Bristol and start an uprising against the English, then march onwards to London, but adverse weather and tides forced the fleet to turn around and attempt a landing on the coast of Wales. The invasion soon lost momentum when the invaders discovered a supply of wine (a Portuguese ship had just grounded, loaded with alcohol) and the invasion petered out in a drunken orgy. The local heroine of the invasion was Jemima Nicolas who, with her pitchfork, single-handedly rounded up twelve of the French invaders who, it is thought mistook her, in her Welsh local dress of a tall black hat and red cloak, for a British grenadier.

Gerald does not mention Fishguard, and must have passed it by. However he probably did pass through Nevern. Llanhyfer Castle is located at Nevern and Gerald tells us that it was, at the time, one of the strongest strongholds in Cemais. Now little remains of the fabric save for an overgrown area at top of the hill above Nevern village. However, what is still there is sufficient to show how significant the size of the castle and its bailey would have been. At the western end of the bailey, which would have been very substantial, is a large motte. The site is now surrounded by trees. There is a secondary motte at the other side of the bailey. Whilst there some traces of rock it is difficult to determine whether these are natural features or part of the original fortifications themselves. Gerald gives us a little of contemporary history in respect of the castle. It had been in the hands of the Fitzmartin family. The Lord Rhys had made peace with the family, sealed by the marriage of William Fitzmartin with his daughter Angharad. However in 1191, three years after our journey, Rhys, after a siege, captured Lhanhyfer castle, urged on by his son Gruffudd, a 'cunning artful, man' in contravention of his word and oaths to William. Rhys then handed over the castle to his son Gruffudd despite his previous oath that he would not hand over the castle to him. Gerald reminds us that only problems follow gains achieved by underhand means. Gruffudd, thanks to the intervention of God, lost the castle and it passed into the hands of his brother Maelgwyn. Lord Rhys, Gerald tells us, decided to disinherit his daughter, his grandsons and grandaughters. Presumably to avoid this financial disaster his sons Maelgwyn and Hywel Sais gave battle and seized Rhys, incarcerating him in Llanhyfer. This Gerald regards as justice for Rhys not holding true to his oaths and 'God took vengeance on him in the most apposite way, for, as he well deserved, he was disgraced and discountenanced in the very place where he had perpetrated a base and shameful crime.' What is more, he had also stolen Saint Cynog's torque and hidden it in Dinefwr castle, so really he deserved all that was coming to him. However, Hywel soon relented and released his father.

The Lord Rhys, the following year, captured and imprisoned two of his other sons. His sons must have been a headache to him and these various activities only go to show that you should keep to your oaths, but they also highlight the unrest in Wales prevailing in Gerald's time with the conflicts primarily between the Welsh and the Norman-English, but even the struggles for power between the Welsh princes themselves. The castle of Nevern was abandoned by Rhys's descendants after 1197 and fell, eventually, into the ruins we see now. Rhys, it may be recalled, was described by Gerald as a man very open in his behaviour and a man of great natural kindness, particularly to Archbishop Baldwin. His behaviour, unless this was normal for the time, does not entirely seem to fit into this category with breaking of oaths, warfare and mayhem and, to cap it, a fairly disfunctional family!

Nevern, apart from the stronghold was also on one of the pilgrimage routes to St David's. The church of St Brynach, which was founded in the sixth century, was in existence in Gerald's day. The present church boasts a Norman tower but the rest of the church dates from 1425–1525 with alterations in 1864 and subsequent repairs. It is nevertheless of great interest and some of the artefacts would have existed in the twelfth century. There are several stones and inscriptions of great antiquity. Inside the church there is a stone, which dates to the fifth century, inscribed '(The Monument) of Maglocunus (Maelgwyn) son of Clutorius', and there is a cross stone inscribed with an intricate cording design. Outside there is another monument stone from the fifth century inscribed to Vitalianus, an incised stone showing faint letters, and on the east wall an incised cross which is a consecration cross for the church. Finally outside is the great Celtic cross which is a perfectly conserved even though it stands in the open and has been beaten by the elements for hundreds of years.

There is a similar cross at Carew near Lamphey. They both date from the tenth or eleventh centuries, are carved on all four sides and stand some 4 metres high. The Nevern cross has a beautiful red colouring on one side due to weathering. It is said that on 7 April each year a cuckoo used to perch on the cross and the saying of Mass was delayed until the call of the bird was heard. One year the cuckoo was late and hardly able to make his call; shortly after he died. The Mass must have been late that year, as was the cuckoo!

On leaving the church, up the nearby hill there is also a pilgrim's cross which has been cut into the living rock over a kneeling recess with a further small cross reminding us that we are on the original pilgrimage route to St David's.

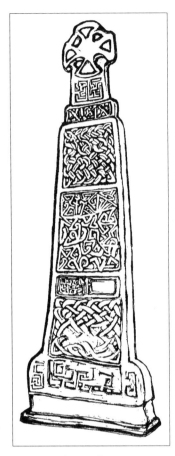

Carew Cross,
Pembrokeshire

The party rested the night at St Dogmaels abbey near Cardigan on the night of Tuesday 27 March, in very comfortable lodgings. The present remains of the abbey are those based on the foundation by Robert Fitzmartin of Cemais in 1120. Despite St Dogmaels being on the borders between the Norman part of Wales and the domain of Lord Rhys, with all the consequent border fighting involved, construction of the buildings had proceeded undisturbed so that when Gerald arrived, the claustral buildings and the nave of the abbey church were probably complete.

The foundations of the abbey can be clearly seen and the habits and life of the monks in the abbey can be envisaged, not least in their hygiene, and there are the remains of an old basin in which the monks would have washed prior to eating. The infirmary and part of the walls of the original twelfth century church are clearly visible.

After resting the night they went across the river to Cardigan into the territory of Lord Rhys and were entertained by him. Both Baldwin and Gerald preached 'to great effect', with Rhys and his sons Maelgwyn and

Gruffudd on the Cemais side of the river. Such was the power of the sermons that apparently many people signed up to take the cross. It was obviously an emotional occasion as one woman gave thanks that, despite her old age and dependency on her son for care, her son had signed up as it was the culmination of her ambition that he should give himself to God. On the other hand there was a contrary experience as another woman grasped her husband's cloak and forcibly restrained him from taking the cross as she had dreamt that the person most dear to her would be taken away from her. She and her husband both went to sleep that night. Sadly she rolled over on to her little boy, who was in bed with them, and he was smothered by her. Her husband went to the Bishop to explain how his wife had been punished for not allowing him to take the cross and agreed now to do so. This time it was without an objection from his wife who even sewed the cross onto the shoulder of his dress with her own hands. So the story ended well, apart from the poor child and the grief of his parents. Gerald tells us that a chapel was laid out in a green field by the bridgehead where the sermons were preached. Subsequently many of the sick who visited the site were miraculously cured, but Gerald does not tell us in detail of the nature of the miracles. Hoare says that in his day there was a site still called Chapel Field – but it has now been buried under an industrial estate.

Chapter 16
Afon Teifi, Cardiganshire and Newcastle Emlyn

Below Cardigan flows the Teifi and it was because of the river that Cardigan grew, based on its strategic position as a port, from the Middle Ages. Above the river stand the remains of the castle built in 1100 by Gilbert de Clare.

Cardigan was the site of considerable conflict, the town frequently changing hands between the Normans and the Welsh. At the time of Gerald's visit it was the stronghold of Lord Rhys. The party probably spent two nights at the castle as his guests. Lord Rhys had taken possession of the castle following his victory over the English at the battle of Crug Mawr in 1136. In this battle he defeated Stephen, constable of Cardigan castle, Robert FitzMartin, and – demonstrating how inter-related everyone at that time seemed to be – Gerald's two uncles William and Maurice FitzGerald. The castle remained in Rhys's hands until his death in 1197 when his two sons, in pursuit of their inheritance, as mentioned earlier, fought each other with Maelgwyn surrendering his brother Gruffudd to the Normans and selling Cardigan castle to King John! But all of Lord Rhys's life was not just in armed battle and warfare as it is said that he was responsible for commencing the first grand battle of words in Wales. He hosted the first National Eisteddfod in 1177. The *Welsh Chronicle* tells us that Rhys had a great feast:

> Rees caused all the poetes of Wales (which are the makers of songs and recorders of gentlemen's petegrees and armes, of whom everie one is intituled by the name of Bardh, in Latine Bardus) to come thither, and provided chaires to be set in his hall,

where they should dispute together, to trie their cunnung and gift in their faculties, where great rewards and rich gifts were appointed for the overcomers; amomgst whome they of North Wales wan the price, and among the musicians Reese's own household men were counted best.

No doubt they were surprised winners! But let us return back to the topography. Gerald points out the big hill, Crug Mawr, where the battle of 1136 was fought, where 'Gruffydd, son of Rhys ap Theodor . . . by a furious onset gained a signal victory against the English army'. They rode past this, to their left, shortly after leaving Cardigan on their way to Lampeter. He tells us that there is a tumulus at the top of the hill that changes its size to that of any who go there. The locals of his time also maintained that if anyone were to leave their arms there in good condition in the evening those same arms would be destroyed at the onset of morning.

Returning to the Teifi, Gerald tells us that it is stocked with the best salmon in Wales and that it was the only river where beavers abounded. He tells many stories about beavers and their perceived habits and how they made their dams and homes. He also tells of their weird habits when attacked. In his words:

Beavers construct holes in the banks of rivers in order thus artfully to elude the stratagems of the well armed hunter, who is watching them from the opposite banks of the river. When the beaver finds that he cannot save himself from the pursuit of the dogs who follow him; that he may ransom his body by the sacrifice of a part, he throws away that, which by natural instinct he knows to be object sought for, and in the sight of the hunter castrates himself, from which circumstance he has gained the name of Castor; and if by chance the dogs whould chase an animal which had been previously castrated, he has the sagacity to run to an elevated spot, and there lifting up his leg, shews the hunter that the object of his pursuit is gone . . . Thus, therefore, in order to preserve his skin, which is sought after in the west, and the medicinal part of his body, which is coveted in the east, although he cannot save himself entirely, yet by a wonderful instinct and sagacity he endeavours to avoid the stratagems of his pursuers.

The concept of a number of beavers cocking their legs at the hunters conjures up a remarkable picture in one's mind. Cardigan boasts more recently of being one of the last bastions of the river otter, which may well also have existed at Gerald's time. There is a sculpture on Prince Charles Quay in the form of a life-sized otter, which was unveiled by Dr. David Bellamy, the botanist, in 1988.

From Cardigan Gerald's route cuts inland past the castle of Cilgerran. This stands high above the confluence of the rivers Teifi and Plysgog overlooking a steep gorge. The earliest castle was probably built by Gerald of Windsor in about 1108 to protect his northern flank against Welsh incursions from Powys. It was built in the form of a ringwork castle using the natural features of the gorge as defences with its entrance being defended by a fortified gatehouse. The present remains are from both the thirteenth and fourteenth centuries. The location of the castle is both spectacular and romantic and one looks down from the battlements to the rivers far below. But more importantly, from Gerald's point of view, the castle is part of his family history, as Gerald of Windsor, the builder of the palace was his grandfather through his marriage to the Princess Nest in about 1100. Nest was sister of Gruffudd, prince of Deheubarth, who was father to Lord Rhys, Gerald's uncle. Gerald certainly came from an aristocratic Welsh family! The Rev. Evans quotes from an ancient book on heraldry which suggests that 'A Welsh gentleman will climb up by the ladder of his pedigree into princely extraction: and that it may be said, Men are made heralds in other countries, but born so in Wales.' However, it is clear in Gerald's case he was there at the top from the beginning!

The story of Nest and Cilgerran castle bears a few moments' diversion. As has been mentioned, she was in her own right a princess and was also renowned for her beauty and was thus quite a catch for Gerald of Windsor. We are told in *Brut y Twysyogyon* ('Chronicle of the Princes') that she was abducted from the castle of Cenarth Bychan, which is probably the castle of Cilgerran, in 1109 by her second-cousin Owain ap Cadwgan. The chronicle relates that when:

> Owain had heard that Nest was in the castle, he went with but a few men in his company to visit her as a kinswoman. And after that he came of a night to the castle and but few men with him, about fourteen, unknown to the keepers of the castle. And then he came to the chamber in which Gerald and Nest were sleeping. And they raised a shout around and about the chamber in which Gerald was, and kindled tapers and set fire to the buildings to burn them. And when he heard the shout, Gerald awoke, not knowing what to do. And Nest said to him 'Go not out to the door, for thine enemies await thee, but follow me.

And so he did. She led him to the privy, or lavatory, which adjoined the chamber and there, it is said, he escaped by way of the privy hole. I am not sure that one would want to give chase after that but then, smells were different in those days. When Nest knew that he had escaped, she cried out from within and said to the men who were outside, 'Why do you cry out in vain? He whom you seek is not here. He has escaped'. When they did not find him, they seized Nest and her two sons and her daughter (this was Angharad, our Gerald's mother) and another son of his by a concubine, and they sacked and plundered the castle. Nest is reputed to have said to Owain, 'If thou wouldst have me faithful to thee and keep me with thee, have my children escorted to their father'. This may have been guile or a desire to stay with Owain, but whichever she had in mind Nest had quite a reputation. She allegedly was mistress to a number of lovers, including King Henry I, earning herself notoriety as 'Helen of Wales' recalling the beauty and activities of Helen of Troy! Gerald does not mention the exploits of his grandmother in his account, probably for obvious reasons.

The travellers followed the pleasant Teifi valley coming to Cenarth Mawr, where Gerald reminds us that Saint Llawddog had lived. He is said to have hollowed out a hole on a point of rock and which now harbours a fishing station. This is part of a lovely stretch of water whence the Teifi runs down an impressive rocky staircase which, save for the changes wrought through the constant attrition of the river, must have been the staircase which inspired Gerald to tell of the salmon leaping up the river, one leap being the height of the longest spear:

> Fish of this kind; naturally swimming against the course of the river (for as birds fly against the wind, so do fish swim against the stream), on meeting with any sudden obstacle, bend their tail towards their mouth, and sometimes, in order to give a greater power to

their leap, they press it with their mouths, and suddenly freeing themselves from this circular form, they spring with great force (like a bow let loose) from the bottom to the top of the leap, to the great astonishment of the beholders.

Gerald's word picture sums up this scenic stretch of the river and it is easy to imagine the hard-working salmon ascending the staircase with their great effort. Gerald mentions that there is a church dedicated to the saint, a mill and a small garden, and so there are, though not the buildings and gardens Gerald would have seen. Below the salmon leap there is an attractive bridge, built in 1787, with an unusual design of large holes under the road level to allow high flood waters to pass through, as well as under, the arches of the bridge thus enabling it to stand the very high water pressure.

The church is of a more recent date, namely 1872, but inside is preserved from early times a memorial, the 'Sarson Stone', which bears an inscription 'Curcagn – filiandagelli' which is interpreted as Carcagnus, son of Andegilli. Below the bridge can be found an old spring or well which has been dedicated to Saint Llawddog and it is reputed that it has never ceased its flow.

Until recently coracles were used on the Teifi in this area for fishing and netting, such use dating back to Gerald's time and much before. A medieval traveller in Wales, some 800 years ago, recorded that he had seen coracles and coraclers and marvelled at the boats 'made of twigs, not oblong nor pointed but almost round, or rather triangular, covered both within and without with raw hides'. There is a small but informative Coracle Centre near the bridge.

The road follows along the river valley up to Lampeter passing through Newcastle Emlyn. There are remains of a 'new' castle at Newcastle Emlyn, but according to the

Coracle

records its founding dates back to about 1240 by Maredudd ap Rhys, who constructed a timber and earth castle. This therefore postdates Gerald's visit by some fifty years. Presumably the name he uses for the town implies that there was some fortification there, the remains of which have been subsumed into the 'new' new castle or lost in time or that there was a newer new castle in the same place. Or perhaps he has incorporated the new name into his account. Whatever the dating the present castle is built on a fine defensive hill above a large oxbow formed by the river way below it.

In 1718 the first printing press in Wales was set up in Newcastle Emlyn by Isaac Carter. This is commemorated by a plaque which was unveiled in 1912 by the then headmaster of the Grammar School. Carter moved on to Carmarthen, where he apparently created another Welsh first by printing the first two-colour page in Wales.

The second achievement of the town is perhaps more fascinating: the last duel in Wales was fought in Newcastle

Emlyn on Saturday 10 September in 1814.

After Newcastle Emlyn the valley continues up to the valley of the Teifi, gaining in height and surrounded by quite hilly countryside until reaching Lampeter, where the party stayed the night of Friday 1 April.

Chapter 17
Lampeter, Strata Florida,
Llan-ddewi Brefi and Saint Padarn the Great

The following morning was quite a big day in Lampeter, judging by the number of sermons that were preached. First the Archbishop spoke, followed by Gerald. Then two Cistercian abbots preached, namely John of Whitland abbey and Seisyll of Strata Florida. The latter two had been with the party on the complete journey so far and continued on with Baldwin and Gerald into north Wales. Whether the congregation was overwhelmed by the quality or quantity of the sermons is not recorded but, for whatever reason, many are recorded as having taken the cross. Lampeter is now a pleasant university town.

The original name of Lampeter stems from Llanbedr Pont Steffan, or Llanbedr Talybont Steffan, which mean the church of Saint Peter at the end of Stephen's bridge. There was a small motte-and-bailey castle in Gerald's time, now a small mound in Lampeter University grounds. W. J. Lewis, a local historian, does not think Gerald and the Archbishop were necessarily put up in the castle. As he writes, 'While in the town he may have lodged at the Priory, a building that, according to tradition, stood on the site now occupied by Temple Terrace and Shiloh Chapel. The evidence of such a place is slim!' Wherever they stayed, they set out the next day for the abbey of Strata Florida through Llan-ddewi Brefi.

The record of the journey then follows a strange route as Gerald seems to come back to Llan-ddewi Brefi after Strata Florida, thus putting an unnecessary twenty miles onto his journey. This is somewhat in conflict with his statement that he left Strata Florida with the Pumlumon Hills on his right, which would have been much more logical as he proceeded on to Llanbadarn Fawr. To go back he would have had the hills behind him. Perhaps he mixed up the order of the villages when reconstructing his journey from his notes, but this would have been a fairly major error and thus unlikely. Another possibility may be that they had to retrace his steps to meet up with Cynwrig ap Rhys, son of the Lord Rhys and his friends, who were signed up for the cross. Or perhaps Hoare's theory is correct when he states that the party returned to Llan-ddewi Brefi and then went down to Llanbadarn Fawr, because the party expected to get a more comfortable night at Strata Florida than at Llanddewi Brefi.

Whichever was right, we will follow the logical route and come first to the village of Llan-ddewi Brefi. Recalling a miracle which is said to have occurred there, Hoare quotes the historian Cressy:

> When all the fathers assembled enjoined David to preach, he commanded a child which attended him, and had lately been restored to life by him, to spread a napkin under his feet, and standing upon it, he began to expound the gospel and the law to the auditory: all the while that this oration continued, a snow-white dove descending from heaven, sate upon his shoulders, and moreover the earth on which he stood raised itself under him till it became a hill, from whence his voice, like a trumpet, was clearly heard and understood by all, both near and far off, on the top of which hill, a church afterwards built and remains to this day.

The church of St David still stands up above the village on a small hill. Gerald tells us that the occasion of St David's speech was that of a great synod called in about 519 to refute

Pelagianism and to enforce greater discipline in the church. Pelagianism, briefly, was a religious view that original sin did not exist and that man was capable of deciding good and evil without divine intervention or, presumably the intervention of the church, which, of course, ran contrary to the Catholic doctrine that man was born into original sin. To accept Pelagianism would have substantially reduced the power base of the church and the Pope. Interestingly, some parts of Lutherism 1,000 years later do not seem so very far away from the Pelagian doctrine.

David was elected Archbishop by acclaim. Presumably the miracle had helped him in his election, and as a result the metropolitan see was transferred from Caerleon to St David's. This story strengthened Gerald's claim that the Archbishopric of a free Wales should be reinstated. Inside the church are various crosses that date back to David's time. There is an Ogham inscribed cross, somewhat mutilated, perhaps at the synod, as it may have been the tombstone of a Pelagian Christian, and the writing is in Ogham which is a particular type of Irish writing. There is a later carving with a cross on the reverse side. Amongst several crosses and stones there are remains of the Idnert stone, some of it broken up to be used in the fabric of the church in the nineteenth century. However, an Edward Llwyd in 1698 made a copy of the Latin inscription on the stone, which is translated as 'Here lies Idnert son of Jacobus who was slain because of the plunder of the Sanctuary of David'. It is important as a document from the seventh century, being the earliest written evidence of St David's life.

As to the structure of the church, it has a strong central tower dating from Gerald's time, and a strong barrel vault dating from the twelfth century. The vaulted ceiling has five holes for five bells in the roof. The rest of the church dates from the 1800s as part of the nave fell down and the rest was replaced due to disrepair. There is a story concerning a great ox horn which was kept in the chancel for many years. Allegedly two oxen carried the stones to be used in the building of the church. They were always overloaded and one died because of the burden. At that point the other oxen bellowed nine times causing the nearby Foelallt hill to split open creating a far more level path so the rest of the task could be carried out with greater ease. We have also seen at Glascwm that the miraculous bullocks were said to have hauled over two bells for the church, as well as a *bangu*. Presumably that was before the death of one in the church building! Llan-ddewi Brefi was a place of upwardly mobile hills and downward created valleys.

The party continued up the Teifi valley, passing Tregaron where there is an interesting church tower, and reached the abbey of Strata Florida. In fact there are two sites of the abbey within two miles of each other. The earliest dates back to 1164 and was built down by the flood plains near the Fflur brook. There are no remains and the present abbey farm probably covers the site. There is a possibility, based on hearsay, that the foundations of a modest abbey church may still be there waiting for archaeological research. Presumably most of the stone was removed to the higher ground to construct the new abbey church, where building commenced in 1184. It is recorded that this new abbey church was opened to the Cistercian community on the eve of Whit Sunday 1201.

But in 1188 which abbey would have sheltered Gerald for possibly three days (3 to 5 April) in the fine accommodation to which Hoare refers? One assumes that the infrastructure was in place at the new location for the monks to continue their devotions and work close to the site and that only the abbey church needed completion, so that they would have been at the new site.

The name of the abbey is derived from the Vale of Fflur (the vale of flowers) and obviously not from the temperate zone of Florida in the United States. Indeed the new location is deep in the country at some height, which would have been fairly breezy and cold, especially in the winter. Sir Richard Hoare found it:

> a situation admirably adapted to the severe and recluse order of Cistercians: surrounded on three sides by mountains many of which still retain their sylvan clothing, open only to the west. The relics of this once-celebrated abbey are now trifling, but time has, fortunately for the lovers of antiquity, spared a most beautiful specimen of its architecture: a very rich Saxon doorway differing in its patterns from any I have ever met with.

Norman gateway, Strata Florida

The abbey suffered very significantly in the dissolution under Henry VIII. It must have been richly decorated, as shown in some of the remnants, particularly in the door leading into the abbey itself with its continuous roll mouldings and spiral motives, and in the remains of the floor tiling which must have spread throughout the abbey. The house was involved in the production of many manuscripts and it is from one of these manuscripts that the opening of the church in 1201 is recorded. It has been noted that it was a hospitable place, earning its wealth from the rearing of sheep, agriculture and from fish, which were also introduced from the abbey to several lakes in the area. The Cistercians, we are told by Gerald:

> (although themselves most abstemious) incessantly exercise, more than any others, the acts of charity and beneficence towards the poor and strangers; and because they not live as others do upon fixed incomes, but depend only on their labour and fore-thought for their subsistence, they are anxious to obtain lands, farms and pastures, which may enable them to perform these acts of hospitality.

He also tells us that when you place the Cistercians in:

> a barren desert [such as Strata Florida] and a solitary wood; yet in a few years, you will find them in possession of sumptuous churches and houses, and encircled with an extensive property.

So successful were they that, in Gerald's time, they were banned from acquiring any more land. At Strata Florida recent archaeological research has revealed that the boundary wall to their immediate farming area was a quarter of a mile away! It must have been most upsetting to the Cistercians that in 1196 disorderly conduct broke out amongst the lay brothers, probably brought on by excessive beer-drinking, and this led, after investigation, to a total ban on beer-drinking at all the Cistercian establishments.

Strata Florida was also an important historical location and was dubbed, because of its connection with the Welsh princes, the 'Westminster of Wales'. The remains of several graves of the princes of Wales still can be seen. The earliest to have been buried was Cadell (died 1175), who was brother of the Lord Rhys. Rhys himself, as we have seen, was buried at St David's cathedral. Three of the Lord Rhys's sons were interred at Strata Florida: Maelgwyn (1230), Hywel Sais (1204) and Gruffydd (1201) and his wife Matilda de Braose, together with his and Maelgwyn's offspring. All of this makes Strata Florida a very special place in Welsh history.

Another important grave is that of Dafydd ap Gwilym, who was born in 1320 and died in 1380. He is buried under an old yew tree. He was a famous Welsh poet who was also a habitué of Llanbadarn Fawr where Gerald next stayed. We will come across him again.

Strata Florida's reputation would have been enhanced as the Holy Grail was said to have been brought from Glastonbury to the abbey after the Abbot of Glastonbury had been decapitated on the orders of Henry VIII. The remains of the wooden cup were placed in the possession of the Powell family at Nanteos near Aberystwyth. 'The remaining ancient fragment is about four inches across, made of olive wood. So little is left, because supplicants used to wish to take a tiny splinter home with them. A priest named John Wharton was supposedly cured of severe rheumatism by the Nateos cup in 1957.' (Breverton)

The cup is now said to be in a bank vault. Byron Rogers

says that 'The present Guardian takes it out once a month to supply water from it to those who ask for this. I promised not to use her name, or to give this to anyone who asked. There is just a house, smelling of dogs, in a lane where one afternoon I called and am not sure as what I found.' Whether this is the original cup or not is unknown.

As has been mentioned, Gerald may or may not have backtracked to Llandewi Brefi but he did meet up with Cynwrig ap Rhys, of whom he writes very favourably. He says that 'we', presumably he and the Archbishop, preached in the presence of Cynwrig's father Lord Rhys, and his other sons Gruffudd and Maelgwyn, who vied with each other in taking the cross. (The latter two sons, as we have seen were buried in the abbey at Strata Florida.) The road from Strata Florida descends down the Ystwyth valley until, after a glimpse of the sea, it drops down quickly to Llanbadarn Fawr, now effectively a part of Aberystwyth, although it staunchly tries to maintain its independence from the larger town. The party stayed the night at Llanbadarn, presumably at the monastery of Great St Padarn.

In the morning many more were signed up for the Crusades. Gerald gives us quite an insight into the state of the church in Wales in his times. Llanbadarn Fawr church had an abbot as priest who was a layman, as were many in Wales at that time. Gerald has a rant at the custom of appointing powerful people and laymen as clergy rather than properly ordained and trained clergymen. He states that over time, they, the lay clergy, 'from a desire of gain, have usurped the whole right, appropriating to their own use, the possession of all the lands; leaving only to the clergy the altars, with their tenths and oblations, and assigning even these to their sons and relations in the church'.

It would thus appear that St Padarn's was such a church and that it was in a sad state of repair both in its fabric and spiritually. It had an old man usurping the office of abbot, and his two lay sons officiated in the services. This sad state of affairs had commenced after the death of Henry 1 in 1135 when laymen had brought in their own clergy. The story is told that, in the reign of King Stephen, a well-travelled knight arrived there and was awaiting the arrival of the abbot to celebrate Mass. About twenty armed young men arrived. When the knight asked who was the abbot, he was so surprised to find it was a man carrying a long spear that he gave up his travels and research and returned to Brittany. Gerald at this point says he will say no more, perhaps because he thought Baldwin would do something to correct the position, but as Baldwin was not so inclined, 'we have thought it more prudent to pass over, for the present, the enormities of this wicked race with dissimulation, than exasperate them by a further relation'.

Gerald was very much a zealot in wishing to reform the problems of the church and strangely, during his life, he had to take refuge at another Llanbadarn Fawr, this time near Llandrindod Wells. When on an official 'visitation' of remote Rhwng Gwy a Hafren (now the Radnorshire district of Powys), the locals did not approve of his official visit and did all they could to frustrate him, first by threats, then by showering his servants with arrows, and finally by besieging him in the church of Llanbadarn Fawr. In his book *Gemma Ecclesiastica* Gerald sets out his views in some ninety-two chapters as to how the clergy should behave. It is a detailed exposition on the proper way to administer Communion, and the behaviour of the clergy and bishops, and is full of splendid stories of deviation, greed and taking of bribes by the clergy and how such practices should be amended. He certainly sets out his stall for reform and behaviour. One instance is somewhat amusing and also a picture of what he was up against! He says that:

There was an instance of a priest in the region of Worcester, England, in our own time, who heard through the whole night that section of a song called the refrain, the part which is repeated over and over. It was being sung by a group of dancers outside the church. Next morning when the priest stood at the altar, vested and signed with the cross, instead of the salutation 'The Lord be with you,' he sang out in a loud voice, in English, the refrain 'Swete lamman dhin are' (because the mouth is wont to speak out of the fullness of the heart, and the refrain was impressed upon his mind). These words mean: 'My sweetest friend, your lover desires your favors.' This incident was the reason why the bishop of the place, William of Norhale, prohibited publicly, throughout chapters and synods, that the song be sung for the rest of his episcopacy. He did not want the people to be reminded by the refrain of the outrageous act of that priest.

The present church of St Padarn is in a much better state than when Gerald saw it, with its present building dating from 1257, rebuilt after a fire, and reflects the fact that it was a very rich foundation in its time, being the mother church of what was then the largest parish in Wales. The original monastery was founded by St Padarn in about 597. There is a story that King Arthur once wished to acquire St Padarn's tunic, which he had been given at Jerusalem. St Padarn refused. Arthur returned, obviously fed up, and determined to have the tunic despite this refusal. St Padarn was equally determined and told the earth to swallow Arthur up, which it did, up to his chin. Arthur clearly didn't think much of this. He immediately repented of his demands and begged St

Padarn for his forgiveness. Padarn relented and released Arthur, who then went away peacefully, if empty-handed. St Padarn was Bishop of Llanbadarn for twenty-one years.

The Celtic connections of the church are reflected in two tenth-century stone crosses which until as late as 1916 stood in the churchyard. They are now protected from the elements in an exhibition area in the church. The exhibition also covers some of the history of the church. In the same exhibition St Padarn's history is commemorated in a porcelain relief showing three figures, including the saint, with their hands plunged into boiling water overseen by the king, Maelgwn Gwynedd. The king had accused the saint of theft. It was agreed that if the saint plunged his hands into the boiling water, but was not scalded, he would be deemed innocent of the theft. So he did just that and his hands were not scalded by the water, thus proving his true saintliness. Sadly, the two servants did not have his divine inspiration and their hands were scalded, thus proving their guilt in what was obviously a fair trial!

The monastery in the eleventh century housed a library which was thought to be larger and more important than those of Canterbury or Oxford, and an enlarged facsimile of a page from Rhygyfarch's Psalter hangs on the wall to illustrate this. It was written at Llanbadarn by Rhygyfarch's brother Ieuan, then the priest, in 1079. The original is now at Trinity College, Dublin.

Dafydd ap Gwilym, the poet, who is buried at Strata Florida, was born in the old parish of Llanbadarn, and on the wall is a copy of his poem 'The Girls of Llanbadarn' in which he writes about his visits to the church. He shows his frustration that he is unable to find a parish girl to love:

ni bu Sul yn Llanbadarn
na bewn, ac eraill ai barn
a'm wyneb at y ferch goeth
a'm gwegil at Dduw gwiwgoeth.

and in Sir Idris Bell's translation:

Never was Sunday that passed by
But in Llanbadarn church was I,
To some fair maid turning my face,
The nape of my neck to God's good grace.

But despite all his attempts he was spurned and left with his head bowed and no girlfriend came his way. He was saddened by the tricks of some young girls who he obviously liked but who did not reciprocate the feeling!

Another writer, William Morgan, the incumbent from 1572 until 1576, was very important in Welsh history as he made the first translation of the Bible into Welsh. This was published in London in 1588. It was written in a new scholarly Welsh prose which acted as a guide for writers in the future and was very instrumental in saving the Welsh language from obscurity, just as the first English Bibles had been instrumental in the preservation and development of the English language.

After Llanbadarn Gerald made his way to the Dyfi. He does not refer to the now University town of Aberystwyth. The present day Aberystwyth is a holiday resort and the administrative centre of the Welsh west coast, but it does have a considerable history going back to Norman times and before. It had a Norman ringwork castle which was built in the early twelfth century, which was replaced by Llywelyn the Great. The last castle built at Aberystwyth, by Edward I, once ranked among the greatest in Wales excelling those in north Wales. In 1401, the great Welsh hero Owain Glyndŵr and his small army relieved Henry V of the castle and defended it under heavy siege by the English, but Glyndŵr lost it in 1408. Now the ruins are no way as impressive as the castles to the north such as Harlech and Caernarfon. Partially this is due to the castle's proximity to the sea and the ravages of the weather.

During Cromwell's time it was torn down and the stonework was used by the locals to build their own houses. So, now the remains offer only a faint image of its once impressive past. Long before the Normans began their castle-building program, Iron Age settlers used the hilltop called Pen Dinas to build a huge fortification which is still visible on the skyline as you approach Aberystwyth from the south and a tall obelisk stands on the hill like a tall chimney pointing to the sky. In the town there is now a pleasant marina. There is much to see but, like Gerald, we must leave Aberystwyth to our left-hand side for another day, and move on to crossing the Dyfi.

Chapter 18
Passage over the Dyfi; Cardigan

The party moved north again up through what is now Borth, along a very long sweeping stony beach up to the southern end of the estuary of the river Dyfi. Had Gerald kept to the land the way is fairly hilly, so it is probable that they kept to the sands below the stony beach.

The Dyfi is the traditional border between the 'talieithau' (kingdoms) of Gwynedd and Deheubarth. As they were leaving the lands under the rule of the Lord Rhys he left them to return to his home, having been with them the whole journey through his territories. To the north of the estuary they were in the land of Meirionnydd, ruled by the sons of Cynan. Gerald describes this as a different district of Wales, being the rudest and roughest country with the high mountains of Snowdonia in the distance, probably still covered in snow, with narrow ridges and sharp peaks. He tells us that it is so rough that if one shepherd were to call to another from alternate peaks it would take them a day to move to meet each other eye to eye! Also he tells us the armaments are different from those in south Wales. In the north they wield very long spears to which chain mail gave no resistance but, in contrast the warriors of south Wales carry bows and arrows which they use with great effect against their opponents. However both methods were pretty effective.

The party rowed across the Dyfi. Despite it being a large estuary it is very narrow at the end with sand spits from both banks almost coming together to meet each other at the sea end. Whilst the present day traveller in his car has a much easier journey than Gerald, Gerald had a huge benefit over the present day as crossing the point must have been fairly speedy. Nowadays it is necessary to drive a substantial distance up the Dyfi to cross the river at Machynlleth and then drive some eleven miles back along the north of the river to Aberdyfi, a pleasant seaside town. Thus a few hundred yards by boat, perhaps a little hazardous, compares to a journey of over twenty miles!

After the crossing they came to Tywyn after what must have been, for once, a fairly easy day's travel. They stayed the night at Tywyn. In the town is the church of St Cadfan, a monastery having being founded by him in the early part of the sixth century. This must have been a substantial church in the twelfth century, constructed by Augustinian monks. The village surrounding the church was based economically on a small port. The church lost its tower in 1692 when it collapsed and the main altar was buried under the debris with the later one built in 1736; this was, in turn, replaced in Victorian times. Inside the church there are large Norman columns supporting the church and there are many points of interest.

Firstly the Cadfan stone. The stone has four faces with two inscriptions and two footnotes, all in Welsh. It was carved some two centuries after Cadfan in the eighth century. It is of particular interest as it is the oldest recorded document in Welsh among the early carved stone monuments. St Cadfan moved from Tywyn to Bardsey Island, which became a medieval centre for holy men and a place of pilgrimage. It is thought that St Cadfan's original followers together with some 20,000 further saints, are buried on Bardsey Island. His mother was St Gwen Teirbron who was known as 'triple-breasted'. The reason for this is that in her first marriage she was mother to three saints, St Wethnoc, St Iacob and St Winwaloe, and she obviously required the necessary equipment! After the death of her husband she married Eneas Ledewig (the

Breton) and bore St Cadfan. As if life had not been interesting enough for her, she was twice kidnapped by Anglo-Saxon pirates and carried off to England, but each time she escaped by walking across the Channel to Brittany. In the end she settled in Dorset but sadly was murdered by the Saxons in the mid sixth century.

In the church there are two large effigies. One of them is of a 'weeping knight'. The knight's right eye is black and under certain atmospheric conditions the eye literally weeps. It is thought to be a flaw in the stone which is particularly susceptible to wet weather or humidity. One can imagine the superstitious awe with which this event must have been greeted. It is thought that the knight is Griffith ab Adda who, according to an inscription on the wall near his effigy which is possibly of a much later date, died when seventy years old in the fourth year of the reign of Edward III in 1331. Having survived to that age he had little to cry about!

The following morning Gruffudd ap Cynan, prince of Gwynedd, came to meet Baldwin at Tywyn and begged his pardon for having arrived late to greet him to his domain. The travellers then moved on and were rowed across the Mawddach estuary. This has an even narrower mouth than the Dyfi, but yet again for the modern motorist it is a journey inland to Dolgellau and back along the north of the estuary to Barmouth, a distance of some sixteen miles. It is a very beautiful estuary surrounded with beautiful countryside and the driver can save a little of his journey by crossing over a long wooden toll bridge over part of the marshes.

They journeyed on to Llanfair (*St Mary's church*) where there is a small church with its entrance surrounded by old yews. Llanfair is a small hamlet and it is difficult to envisage where or how they would have stayed the night. No doubt it would have been very different in 1188. Indeed Hoare comments that he hoped Llanfair presented a better appearance in 1188 than it did in 1804!

Down below Llanfair on the coast one finds the old church of St Tanwg literally nestling in the sand dunes at Llandanwg. This now small village was, in the fifth century, one of the best anchorages in north Wales with Bronze Age, Roman and Celtic roads connecting it with the Dee and Severn valleys. Looking down from Llanfair one can see a large sheltered expanse of water with a narrow entrance to the sea and wonder how attractive it must have been to use in indifferent weather. The port was used as a means of pilgrimage access to Bardsey Island. There is no evidence that this was still being used as a port in Gerald's time but it is likely that the area was still important and much livelier than now. Indeed Llanfair might have been the total area including Llandanwg.

The church of St Tanwg is one of the oldest foundations in Britain and it is probable that the original fifth century church, founded by the saint himself, is under the footfall of the present church. The present church was started in the early middle ages and was extended in the fourteenth century. Nevertheless it is a very small edifice in the early style of Welsh architecture of a simple pilgrimage haven. It is situated on a small isthmus at the mouth of the river Artro. It is so close to the sea that in stormy weather the waves, in Victorian times, were said to inundate the churchyard, and the church has several times had to be dug out from under the sand. This must also have been the case throughout its existence. Indeed it is in a pit surrounded by sand banks and work still continues to save the church from sand and sea. There is an interesting lych-gate to the churchyard.

Internally it is fairly plain but there are some interesting stones both lying free and also built into the fabric dating from its earliest days. The Llandanwg stone, which is eight foot long, dates from the fifth century. It is thought that it may have been brought across from Ireland as there is no similar stone in the area. The monument is a reminder of the volume of Irish trade which must have come across the Irish sea to the village. The Equester stone is in the sill of a window. This dates from the sixth century and is named after its inscription. There are other similar artefacts. The church is unique and one wonders whether Gerald was down at Llandanwg rather than up the hill at Llanfair as, whilst he would still have been in the same parish, the location would have made more sense when they arrived off the beach after their day's ride.

Nearby to Llanfair is the Dyffryn burial chamber. This is an edifice which was erected in the Neolithic age, between 3000 to 1900 BC, for the communal burial of the dead. It was originally covered with stones. It is unlikely that Gerald would have been aware of its existence, as it would probably only been a small mound of no significance and it certainly had not been excavated archaeologically in his day. There are many such sites in Wales.

The following morning they set off and met on a bridge, perhaps over the Artro river, with Cynon's son Maredudd, and many took the cross. It was marked by a sign of charity by Maredudd. He saw that one of his retinue was about to have the cross sewn to his very threadbare cloak. Maredudd threw his own cloak around the shoulders of the man, weeping about his poverty, and presumably gave the new cloak to him.

On his way north along the beach Gerald would have passed to his right the high rock on which Harlech Castle was to be built. However there is no evidence that any castle existed there in his time. Had there been a castle there it would have been entirely feasible that they would have rested at Harlech rather than at Llanfair.

In 1283 Edward I built Harlech castle, high on an outcrop of rock. It is a formidable statement of how Edward perceived his power over the Welsh. The castle must have been spectacular when first constructed, as it was covered overall in white facing and must have been visible for many miles. Between 1461 and 1468, during the Wars of the Roses, the castle was beseiged when it was held by its Welsh constable Dafydd ap Ieuan as a Lancastrian stronghold. It remains the longest-known siege in the history of the British Isles, and is immortalised in the rousing song 'Men of Harlech', first published in 1784 as 'March of the Men of Harlech in Musical and Poetical Relicks of the Welsh Bards'.

The castle was also the last Royalist castle to surrender to parliamentary forces during the Civil War.

Chapter 19
Traeth Mawr and Traeth Bychan;
Nefyn, Caernarfon and Bangor

Gerald crossed Traeth Mawr and Traeth Bychan again, one assumes, by boat. The journey inland for the modern traveller is not quite as far round as the previous two estuaries and, as before, is made shorter by a wooden toll bridge. Prior to the Traeths they had negotiated two other rivers, the Dysynni and the Artro. As the Afon Artro was at Llandanwg below Llanfair this strengthens the supposition that they might have rested at Llandanwg the previous night rather than Llanfair. Gerald explains that '*traeth*' in Welsh means a stretch of sand which is covered by the tide but left bare when the tide recedes. So perhaps they were able to cross the sands on horseback rather than need a boat, as the channel for the river does not appear unfordable.

A *traeth* was also a place of danger. At *Traeth Saith* (the sands of the seven) there is a tradition that seven Christian virgins, flying from persecution, were shipwrecked and stranded there. The seven were saved and were all that remained of very many fair maidens who were taken or persuaded to go into Gaul, to better their condition in the times of difficulty and danger, by St Ursula. The legend of St Ursula is beautifully told in the paintings of Carpaccio in the Academia Gallery in Venice. She is said to have taken to her marriage eleven thousand British maidens of quality, all of whom were virgins, besides 60,000 women of inferior rank all of whom, except perhaps the seven, were allegedly massacred by the Huns in Cologne in 383. It was a hazardous time to be a virgin! If we believe the '60,000', most of the womanhood of the fourth century must have been involved!

Gerald mentions two newly-built castles – one Deudraeth and the other Carl Madryn. Hoare was unable to pin point the location of Deudraeth but more recently two possible different locations for the castle have been found. By far the favourite spot is a 'motte' close to Portmeirion village, not least as there is the modern Castell Deudraeth, which may stand on the spot of its ancient predecessor.

Portmeirion village itself is an area Gerald would certainly have taken time to visit had it existed in his time. It is a world-renowned village built between 1925 and 1973 in Italianate style under the instruction of Sir Clough Williams Ellis. His idea was both to enhance the local natural scenery and, within the buildings and architecture, to create a commercial place where people can meet and stay. It came under some ridicule at the time, but apart from being a popular tourist attrraction, with shops and cafés, Portmeirion is now a fine hotel and the guests can stay in the various houses.

The other castle Gerald mentions is at the top of Carn Fadrum, a large hill nearby on which is an Iron Age fort, but on the western edge there is a small fortress whose dry-stone walls may have been a twelfth-century Norman castle, which was built on the site shortly before 1188. This would make it one of the earliest Welsh stone castles, and it was built by the sons of Owain Gwynedd.

Gerald's party then crossed over the Llŷn peninsula to Nefyn. In the journey one now passes the town of Cricieth, which was built in the thirteenth century to support the castle built by Edward I, which dominates the town.

They would also have passed by what was to become the small village of Llanystumdwy. David Lloyd George (1863–1945) spent his childhood and eventually died there. In 1916 Lloyd George became the British Prime Minister and saw the country though to the conclusion of the First

World War; he continued in office until 1922.

High in the hills toward the centre of the Llŷn peninsula can be found another miraculous well, in this case that of St Cybi who lived there in the sixth century. It was noted for its healing powers, particularly for complaints of the limbs and eyes and according to other sources for scurvy, scrofula and rheumatism. It is said that there was a sacred fish in the well which the monks of nearby Monachdy Bach would catch and eat during Lent. Each night they threw the bones back in the well so that there would be another fish the next day. The well was also used for love divination. Girls would spread their handkerchiefs on the water. If the handkerchief moved towards the south, the girl's lover was honourable and true, but the opposite if it moved northwards. We will meet up again with St Cybi on Anglesey.

Gerald and his fellow-travellers reached Nefyn on Saturday 9 April, the day before Palm Sunday. Nefyn is now a small village on a fine sweeping bay, with a fine view of the mountains, the Rivals (*Yr Eifl*). It is difficult nowadays to realise that Nefyn was once the principal town on the Llŷn, being an important stop on the pilgrimage route to Bardsey Island. The pilgrims would have gathered at the village of Clynnog Fawr before their final journey down the Llŷn to Aberdaron, on the western tip of the peninsula, from where they sailed over to Bardsey.

Nearby at Pistyll is a one of the pilgrims' churches, dedicated to St Beuno, which dates from the twelfth century. It would have been known to Gerald. It is a cell with thick walls and a bellcote. The west side is of twelfth-century construction and the east wall dates from the fifteenth century. On the north wall there is a very indistinct mural said to depict St Christopher, the patron saint of travellers. Above the altar window there is a date inscribed in stone 'DDL' or 1050 and a painted word which may be in thanksgiving for some victory distant in time. A plant called danesberry grows in the churchyard, and was revered for assisting the transmigration of the soul, a sure seller to pilgrims. Nearby there is an ancient fishpond.

Whilst considering the pilgrim churches a brief visit to the church of St Hywyn at Aberdaron is worthwhile. A stone building replaced a wooden church in about 1100. The south aisle was constructed in the 1500s and has some ancient artefacts. It a simple structure placed right next to the sea and would have been a peaceful haven before the final journey to Bardsey. It is said that the pilgrims 'sauntered' on their route and it has been suggested that the word is derived from 'sante terre' or 'holy land'; if one saunters a short distance from the church you come to *Y Gegin Fawr* ('the big kitchen'), which was built in about 1300 and where, if you were a pilgrim, you could claim a free meal before your voyage.

Bardsey Island was an important place of pilgrimage. The island was inhabited by an extremely devout house of monks called the Colidei. Gerald records that, either because of the very clean sea air of the island or because of miracles, no monk died unless into considerable old age.

The island was regarded as very holy and was understood to have afforded asylum to 20,000 saints and to have as many graves including, as Gerald tells, the mid-sixth-century St Deinol, Bishop of Bangor. However, 'it would be more facile to find graves in Bardsye for so many saints than saints for so many graves', and the number of saints' graves quoted above must have taken some finding. The island is quite difficult to reach at times, even in the twenty-first century, and the Rev. Bingley, travelling in the nineteenth century, tells us that after beating against the winds and tides for about twelve hours he abandoned going on to the island. To visit some 700 years before that, in Gerald's time, must also have been very hazardous.

Returning to what was once the very important town of Nefyn it is surprising to learn that King Edward I was said to have hosted a round table there for his knights and noblemen, like the mythical table of King Arthur. He also hosted a huge dance and tournament at Nefyn perhaps to encourage the affections of his new subjects and to celebrate his conquest of the Welsh in 1284. On the outskirts of the town is *Cae Iorwerth* (Edward's field), which is reputed to be the site of the tournament. Not only were the chief nobles of England in attendance but also there were also many foreign guests so it must have been quite a party.

The church of Saint Mary's was founded in the sixth century and would have been in existence in 1188 but now it is a maritime museum, thus serving a very different purpose. In Gerald's time Nefyn was obviously a substantial town and he tells us that in the morning after their evening stay Archbishop Baldwin preached and many took the cross. Nearby on a rocky summit is a very well naturally-protected Iron Age hill fort called Garn Boduan. It contains many well-preserved stone houses. There are two freshwater springs nearby and so, unlike many hill forts, it was well supplied with water.

Hoare records, rather disparagingly, whilst confirming its glorious past, that Nefyn was 'a miserable village'. At Nefyn Gerald mentions that he discovered the works of Merlin Sylvester. He appears to have had a great belief in King Arthur and Merlin, but it would need another book to explore the myths and legends of King Arthur and his court and Gerald's conviction of their existence. These had largely been based on the not necessarily accurate, tales and legends constructed by Geoffrey of Monmouth in his *Historia Regum Britanniae* (History of the Kings of Britain) which he completed in 1136. Gerald was, of course, nearer in time to the legends and might have been better placed to determine their authenticity, whatever their truth!

From Nefyn the journey carried on to Caernarfon past the mountains called Yr Eifl and the villages of Clynnog Fawr and Dinas, neither of which Gerald mentions. The church at Clynnog was founded in 616 by St Beuno. It was substantially rebuilt in the fifteenth century to accommodate the huge number of pilgrims who assembled there before the final journey to Bardsey. St Beuno is credited with having raised six people from the dead, maybe seven, and is the only Welsh saint credited with so many. One of those so raised was his niece Winefride, who we will meet at Holywell. Beuno's well at Clynnog had miraculous properties. Those wishing to be cured after bathing in the well would be laid on rushes on a grave for the night, thus recovering. However, John Ray, in his *Itineraries* (1662), reports that this treatment was repeated every Friday for three weeks. Pennant reports on having seen the featherbed on which a paralytic had lain through the night after washing in the holy well, which seems slightly more comfortable. It was also believed that the powdered scrapings from stone columns at Clynnog, when mixed with well water, made an effective medicine for eye diseases.

A legend is told that St Beuno planted an acorn in his father's grave and this grew into an oak tree with wondrous power. One of the tree's branches grew down to the ground and then bent up again. The tree had the peculiarity that any invading Englishman who passed beneath the branch and the trunk would die immediately, whereas a Welshman could pass through safely.

One day when Beuno was crossing the water to preach at Llanddwyn:

he accidentally dropped his sermon book and was

unable to recover it. However, a curlew came, picked it up, and put it on a stone out of the tide's reach. In return for this kindness, protection was granted the bird so that nobody may ever know where the curlew makes its nest.

The present church is a very large one for the area, and remains of the original chapel of St Beuno and of his monastery have been found beneath the present building. The area must therefore have been of some significance in Gerald's time. St Beuno is reputed to be buried in the church. There is an old wooden chest in the church, made from a single piece of ash, heavily protected with iron clasps with a slit for the poor and others to leave their gifts in the top. It was said to have belonged to the saint although it is of a much later date. If any one was afflicted with an illness an offering, normally of a four-penny piece, could be made and the supplicant, if he sat on St Beuno's grave, was said to receive relief. Also bread and cheese were once offered to the saint on Trinity Sunday and in recompense the church was able to claim all calves and lambs that were borne nearby with a slit in their ears. No doubt there were a lot of slits! There is also a stone which has markings on it which are said to be an impression of St Beuno's fingers.

Beyond Dinas they passed through Caernarfon. The castle itself is probably the most imposing of Edward's castles. The building commenced in 1283. It replaced an older Norman motte-and-bailey construction on the same site overlooking the Seiont river mouth and across the Menai Strait to Anglesey and to the open sea to the west of Anglesey. Gerald refers to this as Arfon castle, explaining that is called Arfon as it is the area facing Môn, the Welsh name for Anglesey.

There is a legend that the Emperor of Rome,

Constantine the Great (*c*.272–337) was borne at Caernarfon to the wife of a Welshman, Macsen Wledig. Later in his life Constantine is said to have dreamt of a castle at the mouth of a fair river among high mountains, its turrets adorned with golden eagles. This could have only been Caernarfon! The castle was built on a highly strategic point, which had been recognised by the Romans, as they had built a strong fortification above the present town some one thousand years prior to Gerald's visit. The name of the Roman encampment was Segontium and it gave its name to Caernarfon as, in Welsh, it was known as 'y gaer yn Arfon'. Obviously in Gerald's time Segontium was not as impressive as Caerleon with the remains of its old buildings still standing. Even in his time there must have been more above ground than presently remains. Now basically one can see the footfall of the fort shown through the various foundations. It would have been was a significant military post occupying, as it did, some six acres of land.

The present castle at Caernarfon takes up the whole of the southern aspect of the walled town, the walls still encompassing the old town.

The castle was bordered by the Seiont, the Menai Strait, and the Cadnont. The Cadnont has been culverted. Inside the north-west tower is the Chapel of St Mary which served the new borough of Caernarfon in the fourteenth century, replacing the parish church of Llanbeblig, which was adjacent to Segontium, and many of the vestiges of the original church remain. The 'Hanging Tower' stands by the castle walls and was, together with the nearby Anglesey Hotel, a customs house until 1822. The last hanging to take place in the tower was in 1911 when an Irishman named Murphy was executed for murdering a maid. It is said that when he died the bell clapper in St Mary's church fell off.

Caernarfon was the administrative centre of Edward I's

Wales and it was here, in the castle, that Edward's Queen, Isabella, on 25 April 1284, brought forth within its walls Edward, first Prince of Wales of the English line, the future Edward II. It is said that he was presented at the castle as 'Prince of Wales' as a prince 'that was borne in Wales and could speake never a word of English'. This is regarded by some historians to be a ruse by Edward to make sure that the Welsh did not put up their own prince to defend their own rights. But the pageant in the castle did not stop the Welsh appointing their own 'princes of Wales' and subsequently leading their armies against the English – from Madog ap Llywelyn to Owain Glyndŵr.

Above the King's Gate is a statue of Edward II, erected in 1320. Pennant thought that this was Edward I, unsheathing his sword and 'menacing his newly acquired unwilling servants'.

It was not until 1911 that, under the Prime Ministership of David Lloyd George, the then member of parliament for Caernarfon, that the next investiture of a Prince of Wales was carried out. More recently Queen Elizabeth II invested Prince Charles with that title in 1969. So the history and traditions of Caernarfon span the period from the Romans to the present day.

Within the old walls are many points of interest but one street, Northgate Street, gives a flavour of the past. When Caernarfon was a thriving port the street was the centre of the red light district and its original Welsh name was *Stryd Pedwar-a-chwech* (four-and-six street) – which was apparently the amount aspiring sailors had to pay for a room, a bottle of gin and a woman for the night! Notwithstanding this, the Rev. Bingley in 1814 sums up the town as 'The most beautiful town in North Wales' and Pennant says 'This town is justly the boast of North Wales for the beauty of situation and, above all, the grandeur of the castle', so the writer's enjoyment of the town is not confined just to himself. The town over the ages has had its moments of downside as well as renewal but its location and history takes some beating. The castle's grandeur has been captured by J. M. W. Turner in paintings at the Tate Gallery and the British Museum, London.

Gerald only passed through and did not rest, as far as we know, at Caernarfon. He says that the road was very hard between Caernarfon and Bangor, although it is difficult in the present day to see any particular problem. But they had to dismount and proceed on foot as the going was both very hard and hilly and they must have been some way from the sea. They thought this route to be good practice for their trek to Jerusalem, the Crusade never far from their minds. Hoare could not find the steep valley which Gerald says they passed through:

> but I have since been informed that there is a valley called Nant y Garth ... it is a serpentine ravine of more than a mile, in a direction towards the mountains, and probably that which the Crusaders crossed on their journey to Bangor.

Wherever the valley was it made a big impression on Gerald and he tells us that after climbing through the valley they were very tired. This is the first time he mentions the physical exertions of the journey. Even Baldwin had to stop to catch his breath sitting on the trunk of an old oak tree. Much birdsong was heard and one of his number remarked that the nightingale was never heard in that area. This is the first time in the journey Baldwin tells a joke, albeit not a very amusing one! Gerald retells it in full:

> Relaxing into a pleasantry highly laudable in a person

of his approved gravity, thus addressed his attendants: 'Who amongst you, in this company, can now delight our wearied ears by whistling?' which is not easily done by people out of breath. On affirming that he could, if he thought fit . . . the Archbishop with a significant smile, replied, 'The nightingale followed wise counsel, and never came into Wales; but we, unwise counsel, who have penetrated and gone through it.

It is not recorded how amusing the interlude was but perhaps it was a real comic story from a man who was sober and upright, and it shows that he was human!

They finally came to Bangor, presumably back in breath, and stayed there where they were well entertained by Gwion, Bishop of Bangor. The following morning Mass was said by Baldwin and he called for Gwion and others to take the cross. This Gwion did with extreme reluctance and he was hard pressed by both the Archbishop and others for his commitment. Nevertheless he was importuned, rather than persuaded, to take the cross, which he did, much to the sadness, even dismay, of his congregation. Not everyone wished to travel to dangerous foreign climes, notwithstanding the alleged potential religious and temporal benefits of giving up their home comforts into the bargain.

Bangor was established by St Deiniol in the early sixth century. He formed his settlement enclosing it with a fence of poles driven into the earth with branches woven in between them in what was known as a '*banga*'. Inside the enclosure he built the first church and monastic settlement and it took the name of Bangor. In about 546 St Deiniol was consecrated as Bishop and his church became a cathedral. The church which Gerald visited was probably about the same size as the present cathedral. Much of the present building dates from the thirteenth and fourteenth centuries and some of the tiling floor dating to that development is still in the west end of the northern aisle. An interesting and early memorial is that commemorating a lady called Eva dating to the early 1300s. Eva was possibly the wife of a large local landowner.

The present Bangor cathedral is the owner of a library of over 4,500 books, recalling the libraries of the priories of the twelfth century. These are now housed in the Library of Bangor University College, including a fourteenth century Pontifical belonging to then bishop, Anian.

The following day they passed over the Menai Strait by boat from Bangor Ferry to Anglesey which is a very hazardous business due to the currents and eddies in the Menai. Nowadays the transit is much easier, using the magnificent suspension bridge built by Thomas Telford between 1819 and 1826 which spans the water from a height of 579 feet. Nearby there is another feat of engineering, the Britannia Bridge, built by Robert Stevenson in 1850 to carry the railway to Holyhead, and, above it, the much more recent Millennium road bridge. The view from the bridges over the Strait is very fine.

Despite the tricky waters as they were rowed across on Monday 11 April, one hopes that Gerald and his party were able to enjoy the crossing.

Chapter 20
Anglesey

The party landed on Church Island and crossed to Anglesey by a causeway. They were met on arrival in Anglesey by Prince Rhodri and all the inhabitants of the island, as well as many from the mainland. Confessions were held in a natural amphitheatre close to the shore. Hoare tells us:

> That from tradition and memorials still retained, we have reasons to suppose, that they met in an open place in the parish of Landysilio, called Cerrig y Borth.

This location was commemorated by the inhabitants in honour of that day, by calling the rock where the Archbishop stood, Carreg Iago, and the stone where Rhodri stood, Maen Rhodri.

Archbishop Baldwin preached, as did the abbot of Strata Florida, and Alexander the archdeacon of Bangor cathedral acted as interpreter. Many of the locals were convinced to take the cross. But all did not go entirely well, as despite the eloquence of the speakers, particularly Baldwin, a bunch of youths from Rhodri's household steadfastly refused to take the cross. However, as so often happened in those days they were to meet with their come-uppance very speedily. Within three days they and others rushed off to follow a bunch of robbers, who turned on the youths, killing some and putting the rest to flight. Those who survived now signed themselves with the cross of their own free will as a result of such divine intervention in saving their lives! In view of the normal lack of resistance to signing the cross one wonders whether the 'thieves' were in fact followers of Gerald enforcing a little authority over the rebellious local youths to encourage their compliance! The sudden change of mind, despite divine intervention, does seem otherwise a little too neat. Indeed divine intervention does seem a little selective in its incidence. Gerald relates that Prince Rhodi illegally took Prince Rhys's daughter as his mistress even though she was a close relation, a cousin three times removed, and his action was held to be incest. Rhodri was advised against such an action by the Archbishop, but took no heed as he hoped to gain Rhys's support, as his son-in-law, against his own brother's sons, whom he had disinherited. In the event these same nephews seized all his lands, leading only to his disappointment at such a loss. Had he been less highly born no doubt he would have been excommunicated for his illegal marriage or had an even worse punishment. Disappointment does not seem very harsh and perhaps this is just another example of there being a different level of pain for the rich rather than the youths of Anglesey.

At this point Gerald decides to tell us more about the glories of Anglesey, apart from its agricultural produce and fertility, which persist today. However, Anglesey would not nowadays be able to provide all the ales produced in the country, even though it was able so to do in the 1200s, from its harvests. The island is fascinating and much has changed over the years since 1188. Certain features remain. Gerald mentions Aberffraw. It is now a sleepy village but from the fifth century it was the seat of one of the three royal palaces of Wales. The palace was abandoned in about 1086. It was rebuilt but came under attacks from the Vikings and now nothing remains. Holyhead was utilized as a port to Ireland as, of course, it still is. At Beaumaris can be found one of Edward I's castles. Nearby stand the fascinating remains of Penmon Priory and beyond at the tip of Anglesey is Puffin Island, a hermit island in Gerald's time. It would be nice to think that Gerald would have visited all these areas during his life. Certainly Penmon would have been a perfect location for he and the Archbishop to visit during their tour, had time allowed.

Penmon Priory marks the area where, in the late sixth century, St Seiriol used to live as a hermit and his well and cell are still visible. There is a fine story about St Seiriol and another hermit St Cybi, whose well we visited on the Llŷn peninsula. St Cybi had his cell, and had obviously moved from the Llŷn, at Holyhead. It would seem that from time to time the two hermits would meet in the middle of Anglesey to discuss whatever hermits used to discuss, presumably survival and religious matters rather than how the local football teams were progressing. St Seiriol would walk to the centre of the island with his back to the sun in the morning and would return, with the sun still at his back, in the evening. He became known as Seiriol the Pale whilst Cybi, as he was constantly walking to the rising or setting sun, was known, by reason of his tan as Cybi the Golden. St Seiriol was buried on Puffin Island, also known as Priestholm, where there are remains of a small monastic foundation, but subsequently his body was moved to the priory itself and buried under the altar.

In the priory itself there is much remaining of the stone building rebuilt in about 1140. The central tower and transepts were added in 1160 to 1170 and exhibit some fascinating features which give a clear example of the architecture and carvings of Gerald's times. From the outside the priory does not seem very interesting, but inside it is a revelation.

Very close to the priory is an old dovecote dating back to about 1600. Gerald does not mention the priory but tells us that, in his time, there was a small settlement of hermits on Priestholm or Puffin island. They lived for most of the time in perfect harmony but when that accord was broken a species of small mice appeared on the island which consumed most of their supplies and made a mess of that which they had not eaten. However, as soon as peace was restored the plague of mice would vanish instantaneously allowing the hermits to renew their activities until human frailties intervened again. He mentions that many saints had been buried on the island in addition to St Seiriol and specifically that no women were allowed to visit the island.

Returning from Penmon one now passes through Beaumaris, which, in Gerald's time, was probably just marshland. 'Beau Mareys' in Norman means 'fair marsh'. In 1295 the construction of the great royal palace of Beaumaris castle was commenced by Edward I and whilst it does not have the prominence of Caernarfon or Harlech castles it is of great interest. Had the building work not ceased in 1330 it might have realised the eminence of others of Edward's castles. It is amazing to realise that over 200 quarrymen, 400 stonemasons and 2,000 mineworkers were engaged in its

Beaumaris castle, Anglesey

construction in the years 1295 to 1296. If nothing else this emphasises the sheer size and magnitude of the workforce, both necessary and available, to construct the magnificent edifices of the castles in Edward's time, and, more importantly the abbeys and cathedrals of Gerald's day.

To construct a cathedral, an abbey or a castle and its defences also required a huge and very competent workforce and this brought great wealth to the areas where the artisans were employed. Gerald would have not known the sheer size of the projects which were to succeed him but he was certainly aware of the size and technical brilliance required for the ecclesiastical monuments of his day, especially at St David's.

Gerald relates some of the legends and histories of his time on Anglesey. At Llanidan church there now is a stone which resembles a thighbone and is embedded in the walls. It is known as the *Maen Morddwyd* (the thigh stone). The stone is reputed to walk during the night and return by morning. If taken away from the church it has the ability to return under its own steam. Gerald tells us that Hugh, Earl of Chester, once invaded Anglesey, and hearing about the famous walking stone decided to test the legend. Attaching iron chains to the stone and another large stone as anchor he cast them into the whirlpools of the Menai Straits. The stone was back in position the very next morning. In another attempt a man tied it to his own leg but his leg immediately became gangrenous and the stone still returned. Equally it was rumoured that if a couple had intercourse near the stone its surface showed great drips of sweat, presumably matching those involved by the individuals, but no child has ever been born from such activities at the particular spot. At some time the stone was cemented into the wall of Llanidan church, which no doubt ensures it will never walk again. Llanidan church also boasts a holy water stoup, which is never filled, but has never been found empty.

Near to Llanidan is Bryn Celli Ddu, which would have existed in Gerald's day but which was probably unknown to him. It is a well-preserved burial chamber which was itself built on top of an ancient henge. Its name translates as 'the mound in the dark grove'. The henge was originally built in about 5000 BC with fourteen upright stones, and the subsequent burial ground some 3000 years later in 200 BC. Both would have been the centre for ceremonies and rituals.

Gerald tells us much of contemporary local history. The same Hugh, as of the thighbone, shut his dogs in a church dedicated to St Tyfrydog (no pun intended) and in the morning found that they were all raving mad. Retribution also hit Hugh in the form of an arrow some months later as he was hit in the eye by some pirates from the Orkneys, who were raiding Anglesey led by Magnus Barefoot, king of Norway. They sailed away after Hugh's death. It is interesting to note that threats to Wales were not restricted to the English but also came from the Norsemen. This particular incursion was a mere ten years after Gerald's journey. Earlier Henry II, after a defeat at Coleshill in 1157, attacked and pillaged Anglesey and again the church of Tyfrydog suffered, but not as much as Henry, who was defeated by the locals, even though they were not as well-armed as his army. Gerald comments that both the Irish and the Welsh are more prone to anger and revenge in this life than other nations, and similarly their saints in the next world seem even more vindictive.

Finally in this chapter Gerald gives us some miraculous genetic observations. He once saw a dog without a tail, which had been lost by accident, but, strangely, all its progeny has the same defect in birth. He recalls a knight, Erchembald. Erchembald's father refused to accept him as his son as he felt his wife had been guilty of adultery.

However, at the boy's birth it was found that the boy had a scar just below his nose in the middle of his upper lip which was precisely the same place as a wound suffered by his father in an accident. The accidental wound had become a natural flaw and thus he was his father's son! Further examples follow. A child had a sight defect, similar to the wound his father had suffered in battle, and a queen who had the picture of a black man in her bedroom gave birth to a black son because she had stared at the picture for too long. Finally he quotes a 'well known' case of a man who had intercourse with his wife after seeing a man with a nervous tic who kept fidgeting with himself both in front and behind. Their son, when borne suffered a similar nervous complaint but which man was his father is not explained! So, perhaps, hereditary problems are not just the evils of the father visited upon the sons but are also the cost of too much imagination in their fathers and mothers and whoever happened to be around at the time!

The island of Anglesey was also renowned for its fecundity and Pennant mentions the great resident of Tregaean, a chapel in the parish of Llangefni:

> who lived in the year 1580 and died at the age of 105; his name was William ap Hywel ap Iorweth. He had by his first wife 22 children, by his second 10 by the third 4, and by his 3 concubines 7; in all 43. His eldest son was 84 in 1581, his eldest daughter 72 and his youngest son then only two and a half years old. He was small of stature, of a cheerful; convivial temper but spare in his diet, living mostly on milk. He passed his time in rural employments, and at his leisure in fishing and fowling, and preserved his memory and senses to the last.

Hereditary matters also follow a good and healthy lifestyle but the father must also have had the patience of Job!

Before leaving Anglesey it would be wrong not to mention the most superb views across the mainland from the Menai Strait. Standing on the shore near Penmon one looks up, on a clear day, to see the mountains of Snowdonia laid before one. Sometimes too one can obtain a sublime view of the mountains with the calm waters of the sea, like a mill pond, overlaid with a slight morning mist and the peaks of the sunlit mountains shining above, a sight which words cannot explain. This cannot be captured satisfactorily in paint as the view is so intense and yet fragile although Turner's painting of *Beaumaris Castle* (1835) (Huntingdon Library Art Collections and Botanical Gardens, San Marino, California, USA) gives some slight flavour of the romanticism of the setting.

Chapter 21
Afon Conway; Dinas Emrys

Gerald, Baldwin and the others returned, back over the Menai Strait, from Anglesey to Bangor, and visited the cathedral again to see the tombs of Owain Gwynedd, who had died in 1170, after a prosperous reign as prince for some thirty-two years, and of his brother Cadwaladr who died in 1172. It is known that Owain was buried on the south side of the Norman cathedral's high altar, which is slightly to the west of where the Bishop's throne now stands, and Gerald confirms this.

At Bangor Archbishop Baldwin appears to have used his authority, unlike his lack of action with the priest at Llanbadarn. Owain had committed incest with his first cousin, having married her, and was, as a result, excommunicated by Thomas à Becket, Baldwin's predecessor bar one as Archbishop. The excommunication had lasted until Owain's death and it was therefore inappropriate for him to be buried in the cathedral. Archbishop Baldwin ordered the Bishop of Bangor to remove the body when there was a suitable opportunity, but in any event, as soon as possible. Soon after the visit the bishop did just that. He had a passage made from the vault through the south wall of the building and caused the body to be pushed through this passage into the churchyard, where presumably it was interred again. So where the body finally rested is a moot point. It may also have been moved back into the cathedral in due course. A tomb in the south wall has been identified as that of Owain, but this is thought to be unlikely as that part of the church was not constructed until somewhat later. But, in view of all the activity of pushing the body out of the church and its being brought back in, anything might be possible! Owain also 'left behind him manie children gotten by divers women, which were not esteemed by their mothers and birth, but by their prowes and valiantnesse.' He was a man of many parts and another example of the good air of the region!

Gerald continued his journey along the coast, presumably along the shoreline with the sea to his left and steep cliffs on the other, and would have passed on his right the impressive Penmaenmawr mountain. The mountain has served as a quarry for many generations and thus has slowly been reduced in size. He must have kept below the cliffs as he rounded into Conwy Bay, presumably at low water, to finally reach Afon Conwy and its estuary, as there would have been no road to the seaside of Penmaenbach mountain, the only route being over the Sychnant Pass. The twenty-first century traveller can drive through a series of tunnels through the granite cliffs on their approach to Conwy. However, it is not so long ago that the corner could only be navigated by a single track road clinging to the edge of the cliff, and this is still visible to the sea side of the tunnel. Before that road was in place it was necessary to climb over the Sychnant Pass leaving the sea well to the right, and this too was very hazardous.

The Rev. Bingham confirms this as the road between Conwy and Bangor and calls it a scene of mountain horror, but recalls that the views from the top of the pass down to Anglesey and Bangor were extremely beautiful.

After Edward I had defeated the Welsh at Aberconwy he had the abbey transferred eight miles up the Conwy valley to Maenan to enable his new town to be built – on the site of what had been a Welsh town for centuries. Some of the buttresses and parts of the walls of the church, mainly on the north side of the church, survive from the original abbey but the rest is of more recent construction in the fourteenth, fifteenth and sixteenth centuries, and various artefacts of these developments remain, notably the fifteenth century rood screen.

The real joy of modern Conwy is its walled town and the construction of a magnificent castle following, which was part of Edward I's campaign to subdue the Welsh. The castle was effectively completed a mere four years after the start of its construction in 1283, which was a massive achievement. But, wrote Owain Maredudd:

> in 1294–5, Madog ap Llywelyn, of royal Welsh blood, led a revolt against the castle towns, burning Caernarfon and beseiging Conwy. Edward was trapped in his own castle, cut off from his army and provisions. The proud king was obliged to live on water and a little honey until the danger passed.

The only criticism that has been heard of the building, which is on a rocky outcrop controlling the Conwy river, is that it was built too close to the station! Sadly, over the years the castle and town fell into disuse and it is interesting to learn what Pennant records of its condition in his time:

> Entered Conwy at the upper gate. A more ragged town is scarcely to be seen within, or a more beautiful one without ... A castle of matchless magnificence rises on a lofty rock at one corner ... One side is bounded by the river; another by a creek full of water at every tide and most beautifully shaded by hanging woods. The great hall suited the magnificence of the founder. It is of a curved form, conformable to the bend of the out ward walls, including one end with a large window which seems to have been the private chaple. It extended 130 feet in length, was 32 broad

and of a fine height. The town contains but few inhabitants, a considerable space being vacant of buildings. It has 4 entrances: the upper gate; the lower, next to the water; a portal between that and the castle; and another to the creek called Porth y Felin or the gate to the mill.

The castle and town have been subject to substantial reconstruction, and even though Gerald does not mention the abbey or town in his descriptions, it is a site worthy of its inscription in the World Heritage List as a historic site of outstanding universal value.

Strangely Gerald singles out the Conwy's waters as being fresh. Whether this implies he crossed the river some distance away from the estuary or whether it is just additional general information is conjecture, but why he singles out the Conwy as fresh compared to the other rivers he crossed can only remain a mystery. In fact it is probable that he crossed the estuary towards the sea, as he refers to crossing an arm of the sea to Degannwy and to leaving the Cistercian abbey at Conwy on his right side, presumably unvisited.

There are a couple of fishy stories concerning Conwy. The first concerns a mermaid who was washed ashore by a violent storm in Conwy Bay in the very distant past. She begged the local fishermen to carry her back to the sea but they refused. Before she died, the mermaid cursed the people of the town, swearing that they would always be poor. So, in the fifth century, Conwy suffered a fish famine and many said that the mermaid's curse was fulfilled. Another tale is about a fish famine and the powers of St Brigid. She was walking by the Conwy riverside carrying some rushes and threw them upon the water. A few days later the rushes had turned into fish and ever since they have been known as sparlings or, in Welsh, *brwyniaid* – both meaning 'rush-like'.

He also refers to Dinas Emrys, near the source of the Conwy, as general information, even though it is a considerable distance from Conwy itself. Dinas Emrys is an ancient hill fort situated above Beddgelert built by Vortigern, a fifth-century warlord, as a secure fortress against his enemies. It is also connected with Gerald's obsession with Merlin and King Arthur, and this may be the reason for his deviation. Apparently Vortigern was advised by his soothsayers and magicians to build at Dinas Emrys and to construct there a formidable defensive tower, but it kept on falling over time and time again. So he was advised to sprinkle the site with the blood arising from the sacrifice of a 'fatherless' boy. The fatherless boy who was found was Merlin, also called Ambrosius or Emrys, thus the name Dinas Emrys. The boy pointed out to Vortigern that the reason the walls kept falling over is that they were being built over a pool in which two dragons, one white and one red, lived. On digging down they found this to be true and, naturally, the dragons having being disturbed, fought a fierce battle in which the red dragon prevailed. It is thought that the origin of the red dragon on the national flag of Wales was established by this event. More important for Merlin, he was not sacrificed as intended, and Vortigern named the fort after him and assigned the fort to him. Gerald however points out that there was also a second Merlin, a Scot, who was made mad by seeing a terrible monster, and it was he who made considerably more prophecies than Emrys. In fact the two Merlins may have been the same one – if they had existed at all! But Vortigern certainly existed. Or so it is said.

Chapter 22
Snowdonia

On the journey from about Tywyn to Conwy the party would have always have been conscious of the Snowdon range and its mountains on the right as they travelled north. In particular the view from Anglesey across to Elephant Mountain and the peak of Snowdon is outstanding on a clear day, and one assumes that is was a clear day for Gerald when he records that they 'seem to rear their lofty summits even to the clouds, when viewed from the opposite coast of Anglesey'. The Welsh name for the mountains is Eryri (*the high grounds*).

Gerald tells us that, in his day, there was a remarkable eagle in Snowdonia who every fifth feast day used to settle on a special stone wishing to staunch its hunger from the bodies of dead men from concurrent wars. The rock has a hole in it in which the eagle was wont to hone and clean its beak.

Gerald did not go up into Snowdonia, at least not on this journey, but had he done so his descriptions of the magnificent passes and landscape would, it is certain, have been full and descriptive. We have touched on Dinas Emrys and Beddgelert. Below Beddgelert the Glaslyn river plunges down close to road down towards Caernarfon. The Llanberis Pass and the Nant Francon Pass to Capel Curig wind through rugged countryside flanked by the mountains. The Llanberis Pass climbs up through the remains of extensive slate mining and the Llanberis lakes. The Nant Francon Pass is considered greater in its grandeur, with Lake Ogwen near its summit. Many of the lakes are now dammed and serve to supply the large conurbations of Liverpool and Manchester with water.

It would seem that the area abounded in strong men and women at the end of the eighteenth century. Pennant refers to a celebrated woman, Mararet uch Ifan of Penllyn, who was the best hunter and fisher of her time, and even at the age of seventy was 'the best wrestler in the country'! She was also a blacksmith and a boat-builder, and one of the best harpists in the land.

Similarly the Rev. Bingley alludes to a woman called Caddy of Cwm Glas who bore a beard. She lived close to Llanberis and was capable of lifting a grown man in one arm and holding him over water until he confessed her strength. She was robbed one day, and followed the thief, beating him with a cudgel, until he very sensibly gave back her property. A lady not to be trifled with! Nor was a Foulke Jones to be regarded lightly. He lived near Dolbadarn, and at the age of three fought off a gander and tore the bird into many bits. He subsequently grew in strength and was able to lift up a stone in a building which task had foiled the attempts of several workmen. Foulke managed to fight many opponents successfully and also solved several disputed arguments through his strength. In one case, similarly to Caddy, he lifted a disputant with one hand and held him over a bridge until he agreed to resolve the problem.

Many stories abound of fairies and strange people and creatures in the mountains and lakes. For example there is a legend that in a mountain close to Lake Ogwen up the Nant Francon Pass there was a cave full of massive treasure. It was found by a man, by chance, one evening but as it was getting dark he decided to return home and then come the following morning to see the size of his lucky find. To be able to retrace his steps the following day he dropped pebbles all along his route. Sadly for him, during the night the fairies picked up all the pebbles and he was never again able to find the cave, much to his chagrin and his financial loss. He should not have procrastinated! Also it was alleged that many nights there used to be a coach near to the cave waiting on the road for a man who had entered the cave. It was well lit inside but when any one approached it the coach rushed away at great speed and could not be overtaken. The particular spot had the reputation of being haunted and it is said no man would approach there at night.

Gerald refers to two lakes which he regards as worthy of mention. The first is Llyn y Cwm. This lake, he tells us, is full of three different fish, namely eels, trout and perch, but the strange thing about them is they are monocular, having only a right eye and not a left one. He tries to find an answer to this phenomenon but cannot, only commenting that he had heard of two different places in Scotland where mullet had been found having this same peculiarity. The Rev. Bingley refers to the one-eyed fish but did not see them. Rather more to the point Pennant wryly remarks that when he visited the lake there was no evidence available to disprove Gerald's contentions! Equally in 1931 Ward states that there are no such fish in the lake. The views around the lake are spectacular but the existence of the one-eyed fish must remain a mystery.

The second lake to which Gerald refers is Llyn y Dywarchen (*the lake of the turf*). This we are told this lake had on it a floating island which moved around the lake depending on which way the wind blew. Sometimes the island moved away, much to the dismay of the local shepherds, carrying their sheep away with it. Ward gives a good description of the island:

> This island still existed in Pennant's time, and the astronomer Halley saw it in 1698 and recounts how he launched the island from the bank and swam it out to satisfy himself that it did float. He gives the

dimensions as 6 yards by 4 yards. Bingley mentions it in 1798, when he described it as being 8 or 9 yards in length and having a small willow tree growing on it. The island still exists although it is little more than a yard in each direction.

Hoare also observed the island in his travels. A legend relates to the island, similar to several other lake legends. In this case an exquisite fairy was seen rowing over the lake by a farmer who not unnaturally fell instantly in love and married her. Sadly she made three fatal mistakes which her father had warned him against and so she returned to the lake and was forbidden to walk on the earth again. However she was allowed to meet with her husband and children on the floating island of Dywarchen and to converse with them, but only on the island itself as it was not solid ground.

There is much that has been and can be written about Snowdonia, not least the beautiful area around Capel Curig and the views up to Snowdon itself.

Whether Gerald ever visited Snowdonia is not known; whether he had seen the lakes, or even climbed the mountain itself, must be left to the imagination. Obviously a visit at this time was not on his agenda for raising volunteers for the Crusades. Had he wished to do so he could have reached the mountain range by following up the Conwy valley past Caer Rhun and Llanrwst, but in the event he was to cross the river leaving the mountains behind him.

Chapter 23
Degannwy, Rhuddlan, St Asaph and Coleshill

As we have seen, the party crossed over the Conwy estuary to Degannwy on Tuesday 12 April. Above Degannwy are two small rocky hilltops upon which had been built two mottes by the Normans in 1088, a hundred years before their journey. Little now remains of them as they were virtually completely destroyed in 1257, but the hills remain.

They crossed a plain with the massive granite shape of the Great Orme on their left. On the top of the Orme is St Tudno's church, buffeted by the winds off the sea, which was partly built in the twelfth century and partly in the fifteenth century. It is said to be on the spot where St Tudno was wont to preach.

No doubt they reached the coast by what is now Llandudno, a holiday town, and then passed up out of the valley by the Little Orme. Just outside Degannwy is the site of an old abbey, Golgarth abbey, now a hotel. It was here that Alice Liddell, the muse for Charles Dodgson's *Alice in Wonderland*, was born in 1852 and where she and her family were visited many times by Dodgson. Further along the road the modern traveller can see an imposing Gwrych Castle built into the hills near to Abergele. In fact, despite its appearance as an ancient ruin, the castle was raised as the whim of a rich Victorian in romantic Gothic style, seeking both as a magnificent home in which to live and as a dream of times past and a search for a new age of chivalry.

The party followed the road to Rhuddlan, which, Gerald remarks, has a fine castle situated above the Clwyd. They stayed the night there being well entertained by Dafydd, son of Owen Gwynedd.

The new castle stands proud above the river and looks

surprising, inasmuch as most of lower level of the stone in the fortifications has been removed to supply stone to build the town. However, the castle is still very impressive with its six towers and walls all constructed in red stone, and despite its size, it still seems to retain an intimate feeling.

The views over the marshes below the castle and the plains to the foothills of Snowdonia and Snowdon itself are very fine. However, this is not the castle which Gerald stayed in, as it is yet another of King Edward I's creations, built during the years 1277 to 1282. Edward stayed there promulgating the Statute of Wales in 1284. The statute effectively set out the way in which he intended Wales to be governed for some three hundred years.

Gerald in fact stayed at the old castle which is just slightly to the south of Edward's castle and the motte and the bailey are clearly seen, again elevated above the river, on what is now known as Twthill (*Twtil*). This was built in 1073 by Robert of Rhuddlan in a highly defensive position and even now is a most impressive mound. It obviously had a long life as in 1277 Edward moved his headquarters to Rhuddlan and presumably found the buildings in the old castle of serviceable use before the new castle took over its place.

Slightly further to the west of Twthill a Dominican friary was built in 1258 for the 'black friars', but this has now been completely built over. Also Anglo-Saxon defences have been excavated, emphasising the strategic importance of Rhuddlan during the ages. Gerald tells us that there is a spring nearby which not only rises and falls like the sea every twenty four hours but also changes at other times during the day; but the location is long lost. Hoare thinks that it was possibly at Fynnon Asaph at the now ruined Capell Fynnon Vair, which is also known as the church of St Mary's Well.

In the morning many were convinced to take the cross before the entourage travelled on a short distance to St

Asaph or Llanelwy. Archbishop Baldwin celebrated Mass in the town. St Asaph cathedral is said to be the smallest in the United Kingdom but it is, as they say, perfectly formed. The present cathedral was rebuilt mainly between 1284 and 1392. Gerald's had had some difficult times with Bishop Adam of St Asaph, and he had excommunicated him. This followed an acrimonious battle between them as to whether the parish of Kerry, near St Asaph, fell within the diocese of St Asaph or that of St David's. Gerald told Adam, in typical picturesque language, 'not to thrust your sickle into another man's corn'. He drove Adam away from the parish, and annexed it to St David's where it remained until 1849. Yet again this is evidence that Gerald was not a man to be messed around.

It was said that a mark on a black stone near to St Asaph was that of a hoofmark of St Asaph's horse, on which he had leapt from an area some two miles away. This miracle has been met with some scepticism, not least as it was more a miracle concerning the horse than the saint!

St Asaph cathedral is an interesting building. It has had a chequered career over the years as it was burnt down in 1282 and again in 1402. It has several features worthy of comment. One is the 'Greyhound Stone'. This dates from about 1330 and depicts a greyhound chasing a hare, the image of the hare being the harbinger of death in Welsh folklore.

St Asaph is also a city which long predates Gerald's visit. Pennant records some of its history:

> Fording the Clwyd, I soon came in sight of Llanelwy. The handsome extensive bridge, the little town and the cathedral mixed with trees, form a most agreeable view. When Kentigern, Bishop of Glasgow, was driven from his see in 542, he retired into Wales and

established here a monastery for 965 monks, instituted on the same plan with that of Bangor; part for labour, part for prayer.

A miracle is ascribed to St Asaph at the time he was a disciple of Kentigern. Kentigern was given, in the way of Celtic saints, to pray in icy cold water, presumably the Elwy, below the cathedral. One day having suffered extreme cold from this immersion he asked Asaph who was attending him, to find a faggot with which he, Kentigern, could be warmed up. Asaph returned bringing him hot coals in his apron. Through the miracle of carrying hot coals without injury Asaph revealed his sanctity to all. One hopes that St Asaph's apron was a strong leather one. Because of all these good works and exploits he succeeded Kentigern as bishop after his death.

There is also a story which connects Gerald's grandmother Nest and St Asaph. St Asaph came to the rescue of Nest who, when out one day, lost her ring in the sea, where it was swallowed by a fish. At a banquet her husband, Maelgwn, saw that she was not wearing the ring and was very angry. Asaph learnt the truth from Nest which he believed and told Maelgwn the story but he, Maelgwyn, leapt up, shouting, 'No! I will not believe a word of it. The Queen, to show her favour for some handsome face, has given away her ring and now repents when it is too late. Fool I was, ever to trust her. It is no fish that has her ring nor does it hide in any pool' (Wilkie). They then proceeded to eat their meal and the Bishop prayed with great intensity. Surprise, surprise, a fish was served and inside was found the ring so all ended in happiness – until the next time, for as we have already seen, Nest did not have an altogether unblemished reputation. But this time she survived!

After the Mass they moved on almost immediately to

cover the remaining journey down from the height of St Asaph to near the sea at Basingwerk abbey, with its views over the Dee to the Wirral peninsula and beyond to Liverpool. Gerald comments that the route they took passed through the area of several successful silver mining works. Basingwerk abbey was a Cistercian establishment which had been founded on a different site in 1132 and it was moved to its present location where the house received a significant charter of confirmation from King Henry II in 1157. The ruins show it to have been a wealthy abbey, close to the coast road from Chester into Wales, drawing great wealth from wool, salt, lead and silver. The Rev. Bingley also tells us of the extensive lead mines which were worked in his time.

The abbey is also close to St Winefride's Well, which was under its ownership and protection. Many pilgrims have flocked to the well throughout the ages to cure their ailments in the holy water and to pray for their good fortune. In so doing they would have provided great fortune to the Cistercians of Basingwerk. The importance of the well dates back to a chapel built by St Beuno in the seventh century. It is recorded that, in 1115, the Earl of Richmond visited the well to obtain blessing for his military exploits – presumably against the Welsh!

Bearing in mind the obvious properties of the well in Gerald's time it is surprising that he did not mention it in his book. Perhaps it was so popular that he felt that further mention was not necessary, although he has mentioned other springs on his journey.

The legend of St Winefride is worthy of attention. She was the daughter of a local Prince and her uncle was St Beuno, who we met at Clynnog Fawr. One day Caradog, a local chieftain, attempted to seduce her, but she ran away from him towards St Beuno's church. Caradog was a bit

Winifrede's well

miffed at her lack of response to his overtures so he chased after her and cut off her head (which was a little over the top!). Where her head had fallen a spring of water emerged. Luckily, at the same time, St Beuno appeared from his church, saw what had happened, and placed Winefride's head back on her body, praying for her life. She came back to life in answer to his prayers and lived a long and religious life. However she always retained a white scar encircling her neck as witness to the problems she had faced as a martyr (or near martyr, since she had returned to life). She became a nun and abbess of a community at Gwytherin, where she eventually died and was buried. Caradog sank into the ground and was never seen again.

The well has been visited by pilgrims throughout the years. In 1415, Henry V called on St Winefride's support before the battle of Agincourt, having gone there on foot on pilgrimage from Shrewsbury. The shrine still welcomes pilgrims hoping for a cure or support. In about 1500 the well was covered by the new shrine. This is in the form of a beautiful two-storey building with a small chapel above, in perpendicular style. The chapel is well used, even in this modern age as a place of pilgrimage and prayer. The vaulting and the stone carvings are of great historical interest.

The well did not have only a spiritual purpose as the force of its waters was significant. The Rev. Bingley states that, in his time, it:

> produced not less than eighty-four hogsheads in a minute. The well has never been known to be frozen and it scarcely ever varies in quantity, either in droughts, or after the greatest rains. These circumstances render it of inestimable value: for, although the water has only a mile and a hundred and twenty-four yards to run, before it arrives at the sea, it turned, a few years ago, the machinery to eleven different Mills and Manufacturies.

So it is strange that there is no mention of such a well in Gerald's travels as surely he must have visited it as the party were so close to Holywell or the Holy Well. However Hoare surmises that the miraculous history of the well might have been the invention of the monks at Basingwerk to drum up business and revenues and that it was not so famous in Gerald's time. But this must be incorrect for, as we have seen, many important visitors had sought the benefit of St Winefride's interventions even in the years before Gerald passed by.

The following day, on Thursday 14 April, they set off in some trepidation, to ride over an extensive quicksand to the west side of the Dee estuary. The course of the Dee would have been very different in Gerald's time. It was canalised in the middle of the eighteenth century, to enable Chester to continue as a great port. This action had unintended consequences as the canalisation caused the river to follow a different path, changing its course completely, and substantially increasing the silt deposits in the estuary. So Chester ceased to be a port of any consequence, which allowed the development of Liverpool as the predominant port of the area.

Gerald says that they passed the forest of Coleshill to their right where Henry II was defeated by the Welsh. He was in fact defeated three times, once at Coleshill, once in the south Wales and once in Powys. Gerald blames his lack of success on what may seem very appropriate reasons, even in the twenty-first century, and should be taken to heed by modern politicians:

> In every expedition, as the artificer is to be trusted in his trade, so the advice of those people should be consulted, who by long residence in the coutry, are become conversant with the manners and customs of the natives; and to whom it is of high importance that the power of the hostile nation, with whom, by a long and continued warfare, they have contracted an implacable enmity and hatred, should be weakened or destroyed.

In other words, get the residents of the country you have invaded on your side and you will succeed in the long term. Henry II did not! At the same battle Gerald tells a story of a faithful dog which is reminiscent of Gelert at Beddgelert. A soldier was killed and his faithful greyhound stood watch over the body for nearly eight days without food and defended the body from all predators. In appreciation of the faithfulness of the dog the English buried the Welshman's body with all due ceremony, even though they were enemies and the body itself must have been pretty nasty. What happened to the faithful dog is not recorded, though one hopes that it was rewarded in a more tangible way than being killed. So Gerald and Baldwin came to Chester crossing over a ford across the Dee and arrived on the 'Day of Absolution', Thursday 14 April. They were to stay for the whole of Easter, leaving on Monday 18 April. Again it must have been a much-needed rest.

Chapter 24
Passage over the Dee; Chester

So Gerald, Baldwin and the others had arrived back into England, as they were on the border between England and Wales delineated by the Dee at Chester Castle. They stayed, presumably at the abbey, for the whole of Easter. Archbishop Baldwin delivered some sermons and, as a result, many took the cross. Little remains of the once strategic castle built in the twelfth century by Hugh de Avranches, also known as Hugh Lupus, the first Norman Earl of Chester. The castle controls the Dee, but only two towers, the Flag and the Agricola, and part of the inner bailey curtain wall and gateway remain. It was built in the same red sandstone as the cathedral. There are local tales that in Gerald's day the fords on the Dee changed each month and, depending on whether the ford moved toward England or toward Wales, it could be determined which country was likely to fare best in the war that year. This emphasises the warlike conditions of the times although many of the 'wars' were often merely raiding skirmishes and relatively local.

Gerald reminds us that the Dee rises in Llyn Tegid (the lake near Bala) and that the river abounded in salmon even though they never lived in the lake itself. He points out that the Dee is never swollen by rain but that the winds often make it rise. What with the quicksands, tides, moving fords and winds, the Dee was fairly treacherous. The estuary still is, with the tides sweeping in very speedily to catch the unaware in the many gullies, particularly up at the mouth of the estuary, and many have been startled by the fast approach of the sea especially when walking over the seemingly flat sands to Hilbre island.

The history of Chester goes way back into Roman times and there are many Roman remains in the City. It was the fortress of the Roman XX Legion, the Valeria Vectrix, and Deva, as Chester was then known, was a major port. After the Romans left in about 400 the city deteriorated under Saxon rule so that it was in a sad state by 900. It was revived under the Normans in about 1070. However the Roman walls, albeit modified and modernised, still surround Chester in a two-mile circuit, and it is a pleasant walk around the existing wall, from which Chester can be seen and enjoyed from above.

In 907 the remains of St Werburgh were transferred from Hanbury where she had died in 699. Her brother Cenred, King of Mercia, had moved her body some time after she had died and found the body to have been miraculously preserved, thereby becoming an object of veneration and pilgrimage. The body was moved to Chester for safety during the Viking threat and was housed in a church on the present site of the cathedral. With the body came the benefit

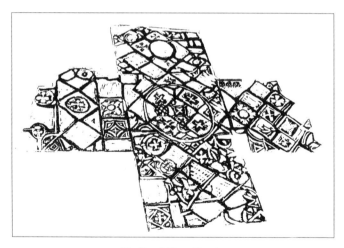

Medieval tiles, Chester

to Chester of becoming a centre for pilgrimage and St Werburgh was adopted as Chester's patron saint, a very lucrative addition to have attained. The same Hugh Lupus who had constructed the castle decided to transfer the church into a Benedictine abbey, possibly as recompense for the riotous life he had led, and asked Anselm, Bishop of Bec to assist him in this task. Anselm arrived in 1092 and he and his monks started the construction of the abbey using the existing Minster as its base.

In Gerald's time the abbey and the Benedictine buildings would have been virtually as imposing in size as the present cathedral, probably stretching up to near the present high altar. However, the cathedral looks very different from how it would have been in 1188.

For example, the nave would have been very dark and have risen to only one storey based on the heavy Norman pillars and rounded arches. It was rebuilt in the lighter Gothic style over the three centuries from 1250 on. It is thought that the end of the cathedral up to just before the now high altar in 1188 would have been apsidal rather than the present square structures. The cathedral was further restored in the nineteenth century under the direction of Sir George Gilbert Scott, as were so many religious buildings.

Internally the cathedral of Gerald's time would have been organised differently with a large rood screen splitting the nave so that the monks could worship in the quire, unobserved by the public in the other part of the nave, and the monks would have entered from the cloister entrance to the main cathedral. All the walls of the cathedral, as indeed would all the religious establishments of Gerald's age, would have been covered in paint and decoration which would have looked garish to the modern eye but very impressive to the receptive medieval eye, teaching the Bible stories through pictures. One can get an idea of the effect of such decoration and its effect through painted surfaces at the cathedral at Albi in France where everything is much as cathedrals must have been in medieval times.

On the floor above the baptistry is St Anselm's chapel or the abbot's chapel. It looks down over the baptistry itself and the abbot, unseen by the clergy and laity, would have been able to monitor all that went on. About half of the chapel dates from between 1160 to 1170 and it has fine barrel vaulting from that period. Gerald must surely have prayed there. This would have led out to the abbot's hall, now an open space, on the first floor level, and to the abbot's house to the left and all the living space of the Benedictine monks. These buildings are now used for offices by the spiritual and lay members of the cathedral. The cloisters are reputably among the best preserved of any English cathedral and were laid out in the twelfth century as open arcades. Gerald and the archbishop would have felt very much at home in such magnificent surrounds although there is no mention of the comfort or the reception they received from the abbot. One can only imagine it to be very comfortable and pleasant after the travails of their journey.

Gerald does not mention the abbey save only to state that Chester boasted of being the burial place of both the Holy Roman Emperor Henry V and King Harold. These comments are based on two myths. Henry V was said to have died in 1125 at Utrecht. Some stories persisted in Gerald's time that the news of his death was untrue and that he had gone into exile, finally reaching Chester. Similarly there were rumours that Harold escaped death at Hastings and had fled to live in obscurity in either Waltham abbey to the north of London or to Chester. Apparently, according to Gerald, the identity of both bodies was only revealed when they made their last confessions. In either case there seems to be no hard evidence; had there been so, there would surely have been a shrine in the cathedral, as magnificent as that of St Werburgh, to commemorate the interment of both the emperor and the king. However, the Rev. Bingley tells us that visitors, in his time, used to be shown an old grave, reputedly Henry's, to the south side of the altar, but he is entirely dismissive of this, stating that it was well recorded that Henry had died and been buried in Liege or Utrecht.

Gerald tells us that the Countess of Chester, who kept tame deer, presented Baldwin with three small cheeses made from deer's milk, shaped in a mould, something he had never come across before. Indeed such deer cheeses are not well-known in the present day, but had Gerald had the benefit of the internet he would have been able to purchase such a product from Wisconsin in the USA! Gerald also, instead of telling us about Chester, tells of some of the phenomena which had occurred in the region in one of his digressions.

Firstly he reports that a stag had served a cow with the resulting offspring a deer-cow. It was 'resembling its mother in the fore parts, and the stag in its hips, legs and feet, and having the skin and colour of the stag: but partaking more of the nature of the domestic rather than the wild animal, it remained with the herd of cattle.' Genetic engineering was quite the vogue in 1188. A further example was the crossing of a bitch with a monkey the progeny being a rather revolting litter of puppies being ape in front and dog behind which were quickly killed off. He also refers to a rather sadder birth of a woman who was borne with no hands and compliments her on the way in which she was able to compensate for her deformity as she was able to use her feet to sew and to use scissors and thread as well as any other women, much to the surprise of all.

After Easter and their stay in Chester they set off again

leaving Chester behind them, this time turning to the south and back towards the eventual end of their journey in Hereford, presumably with the thought that home was in sight.

Chapter 25
Whitchurch, Oswestry, Powys and Shrewsbury

The party crossed over the Dee back into Wales and into Powys. Powys was a district renowned in Gerald's time for many stud farms breeding from horses recently introduced from Spain. The party was met by the princes of Powys. Gruffudd ap Madog, Elise, a number of their followers and many others took the cross. The crowd also included many who had already taken the cross following the separate efforts of Reiner, the Bishop of St Asaph. Reiner was obviously a powerful preacher as once, when he had been encouraging people to take the cross, one young man, whose friends had already signed up, brandished his heavy · spear above his head swearing that he would not sign up until he had avenged his master's death. He waved the spear above his head with such great violence that the spear broke into pieces and fell out of his hand to the ground. He was left with nothing but the end of the shaft. Obviously shaken, he was clearly also stirred, and regarded this as an omen and quickly took the cross before it was too late.

The meeting with Gruffudd was also momentous. He renounced his illegal marriage with his first cousin Angharad before Archbishop Baldwin. He presumably did this to gain Baldwin's pardon and absolution for his transgressions before heading to the Holy Lands. For Angharad, one assumes there was no such comfort, and it could not have been a very good move for her to have had her marriage annulled. Gerald records that Henry II had entered Powys by the same route as themselves, in his case at the head of a powerful army which was beaten out of hand by Owain Gwynedd. Previously Owain had dissuaded his colleagues from deciding to sack English churches on the grounds that by so doing they would be incurring God's wrath, and to beat the English, which they did, they would need all the help they could get, and especially that of God. It is an example of both sides fighting with God on their side (which must always have given God a severe independence problem in applying a just result!).

They passed through the market town of Whitchurch in England before pressing on back into Wales to Oswestry where they spent the night. Whitchurch is a small market town dominated by the tower of St Alkmund's church and owed its existence, in Roman times, to being a fort on the road between Chester and Shrewsbury. When the Lamb Hotel opposite the church was demolished in 1976 remains were found of the Roman town of Mediolanium ('the town in the middle of the plain'). The town was also on the stagecoach route to Holyhead for travellers to Ireland, and was obviously a wealthy town in those days, as is shown by the pleasant Georgian buildings. The first church would have been a wooden church; this was replaced by a stone one shortly after the Norman Conquest in 1066, giving the town of Whitchurch its name. A third church built on the same spot fell down in 1711, and the present Queen Anne structure was consecrated in October 1713.

From Whitchurch the party seems to have taken a somewhat roundabout route presumably so that they could re-enter Powys at a prearranged point to meet Gruffudd, as has been mentioned earlier. Then they would have ridden to the west, passing the meres at Ellesmere and the small castle of Whittington, now attractive ruins.

Finally they reached Oswestry where they were put up and 'most sumptuously entertained after the English manner, by William, son of Alan, a noble and liberal young man'. One gets the impression that this was somewhat of an unscheduled stop, and indeed may be the reason for the deviation from the straight road to Shrewsbury, but it certainly sounds as if was a good party! Julie Kerr, in her research into food and drink in the twelfth century, gives a glimpse as to the sort of evening it must have been. The FitzAlans must have had significant resources; throwing a banquet for the Archbishop would have been a great opportunity for him to have shown off his power and conspicuous magnificence. It would have been much more lavish than even the best hospitality of the various religious houses and castles at which they had previously rested.

The food with which they were served is obviously unknown, but the writing of contemporaries, David of Beccles and Alexander of Neckam, which Kerr quotes, give some fair idea of what might have been available and the splendour and lavishness of such feasts. One report is of figs, pomegranates and gingerbread being served up as tasters. Others talk of wild goose served with pepper sauce for the lords and with salt for the other guests. Sauces could include garlic, and such spices as cumin. There was also an order in which food was to be served. David of Beccles, a sort of early Mrs Beeton, says that pies should be served after meat and fowl, and that these latter could 'include pork, beef, mutton, venison, hare, roebuck and capon. "Soft things" and fried foods were then served to allow the teeth to rest. To finish, diners were brought napkins containing wafers, spices and fruits such as pears.'

When it was a Friday or fast days the fish might include mullet, salmon and conger followed by perch, pike or roach. No doubt this was all washed down with copious alcoholic beverages. After the meal there would be entertainment and finally to bed, usually on the floor of the main hall, but for important guests such as the Archbishop there may have been a separate bedroom to which escape could be made. A feast like these was certainly worth the party deviating, and confirms Gerald's comment that FitzAlan was 'a noble and liberal young man'!

In Oswestry one finds the FitzAlan name everywhere, emphasising the power and status of the family as semi-independent Marcher lords. The FitzAlan family went on to great things in English history, eventually gaining huge swathes of land in Sussex and elsewhere, and the title of Earl of Arundel in the 1500s. Due to the lack of a male heir, in 1580 title and estates passed to the Howard family and the Arundel title merged with the Earl of Sussex, and later was devolved into the Dukedom of Norfolk. So it would appear the influence of an Oswestry family in 1188, which was then a powerful one, grew exponentially, despite some ups and downs, throughout the ages until the present day. It is assumed that Gerald was entertained in the castle. This is now no more than a mound but, in his time, it must have been a much more significant structure. No doubt more were signed to the cross at Oswestry and it is possible that Meurig Llwyd took the cross there. It was through his exploits that the Lloyds of Llanforda were allowed to use a double-headed eagle in their accoutrements, as he had captured Saladin's standard in the Crusades. This double-headed eagle motif can still be seen at the Lloyd's mansion in Bailey Street.

Oswestry is a pleasant town and full of history, although it has suffered over the years. Parts were being burnt down three times in the 1500s and it also suffered during the civil wars. Just outside the centre is the significant old Oswestry hill fort. Within the town there is the old school, a fine timbered building, with close to it the church dedicated to St Oswald, king and martyr. Most of the large church was rebuilt in 1675 and subsequently in the late 1800s, but the oldest part, the tower, dates from about 1085. In the church is the Yale Memorial commemorating the Yale family who are remembered for their foundation of Yale University at Newhaven in the United States of America.

The name of Oswestry is said to have been in memory of Oswald, the Saxon king of Northumberland, who fought and lost a battle nearby to Oswestry in 642. King Penda, his opponent, had Oswald's head and arms cut off and placed on tall wooden stakes and his body taken away to be buried at Bardney in Lincolnshire. The Rev. Bingley maintains that the place where the stakes were planted was called Oswald's Tree and the town thus became Oswestry. Legend has it that Oswald's right arm was carried off by an eagle which dropped it. On the place that it landed a spring bubbled up now known as Oswald's Well. It is close to the church being, as Leland estimates only 'a bow shot' away. Over time Oswald became revered and venerated and his grave became a place of pilgrimage and many miracles were said to have occurred there. The well became also a place where people could get an early diagnosis of their health by throwing one of their garments onto the water. If the clothing floated they would survive but if it sank the patient would die.

Following the night of entertainment, whether with heavy heads or not we do not know, Gerald moved on past Westcliffe, with views in the distance to the right of the Wrekin and Wenlock Edge to Shrewsbury, where they stayed to rest and recover for a few days. But it was not all rest because Gerald and Baldwin preached: in Gerald's case, elegantly, as he says modestly. Many took the cross and the hard decision to excommunicate Owain Cyfeilog was taken as he, alone of all the Welsh princes, hadn't bothered to meet Baldwin and Gerald and they had thus missed the opportunity to convert him and his followers to the cross. Having recorded that, Gerald compliments Owain as being a good land manager as he looked after his affairs sensibly.

He was often in disagreement with his own leaders, was a close friend of King Henry II and would appear to have been a bit of a maverick. He was also able to take the king to task over his habit of holding on to church benefices as long as possible to retain their revenues. Owain must have had a strong character and thought that managing his own estates was more worthwhile than the uncertain life of a Crusader, despite the threat of – or actual – excommunication.

One assumes that they all stayed at the abbey at Shrewsbury on Tuesday 19 April, and possibly for the next three days. The abbey had been built on the site of an old wooden church and was yet again a Norman creation. Roger de Montgomery, whose twelfth-century stone carving is to the south aisle of the church, founded the present abbey. He died in 1094 and was buried in the abbey but the carving is from about one hundred years later. He had been inspired in the task of the foundation by the priest of the old church Odelirius, who had been on pilgrimage to Rome. Roger established a Benedictine house. Monks were brought over from Normandy and the first abbot took up regular duties in 1087. The building of the abbey and all the supporting community buildings would have been completed by that date. The abbey church itself must have been a fine structure, much larger than the present building, and the Norman remains can still be seen in the centre bays of the nave, an archway at the head of the north aisle, the west door and part of the north porch with its barrel vaulting. Like Chester the present buildings give a good idea of how large the religious structures were in Gerald's time. The infrastructure must indeed have afforded our travellers, in its comfort, much respite from their journey and to build up their strength to prepare for the final leg of their long task back to Hereford. More importantly, they would have had a quiet moment to take stock of all that been achieved in the previous weeks. The abbey must also have been a very wealthy establishment as it was on the main road from London to Wales. It had access to the navigable river Severn and was endowed from the start with the monopoly rights from three profitable mills. The abbot was able to levy tolls over Abbey Foregate and exact fines for indifferent produce, and was entitled to a tithe of all the venison in Shropshire, except from the deer which ranged in the woods of Wenlock.

In 1137 Abbot Herbert brought the remains of St Winefride from her grave at Gwytherin and interred them in a shrine at the west end of the cathedral. Nothing now remains of the original shrine, as it was destroyed at the Dissolution, and a Guild, which had been formed in her memory, was also disbanded at that time. So St Winefride, having had an interesting life, faded from sight until in 1987 when the Guild was re-established to support, in her name,

Refectory pulpit, Shrewsbury

the abbey church. A fragment of a thirteenth-century reredos is believed to depict St Winefride along with St Beuno and St John the Baptist. The abbey grounds themselves were substantial, as can still be seen today, although only a fourteenth-century stone pulpit, which was part of the refectory, remains. The font is of interest as it ties in the history of the Roman encampment which was built close to Shrewsbury at Wroxeter. The font is constructed from an inverted ancient Roman pillar probably from the fort. The new part of the abbey was reconstructed in the nineteenth century. The abbey was also part of political history as it was to the Chapter House that Edward I called Parliament in 1283 to try to resolve what should be done with Dafydd, brother of Llywelyn ap Gruffudd, after the latter's defeat and death. The Parliament of 1283 for the first time included some Commoners and could, on those grounds, be called the first 'democratic' parliament. For the record Dafydd was sentenced to death.

Shrewsbury must have been a fine town in Gerald's time, as indeed it is today. It has a castle, the foundation being ascribed to Robert de Montgomery. The castle stands proud above a railway station, just like Conwy, and nearby are the original Royal Shrewsbury Grammar School buildings. The School was founded in 1552 by Edward VI.

After the stay at Shrewsbury of three days Gerald, Baldwin and their supporters set out on the final leg of their journey to Hereford cathedral on Friday 22 April. If they covered the whole distance to Hereford in one day it was quite a feat. Certainly they must have broken off somewhere, but this is not on record, and they were of course travelling this last stage through England with, presumably, no more recruiting to do and no more delays.

Chapter 26
Wenlock Edge, Bromfield, Ludlow, Leominster, and back to Hereford

Gerald's description of the last stretch of his journey is very short and this seems to imply that as the journey was nearly over he had little more to say. He must have wished to get to the end of the journey and return to his home. He no doubt sought to be back to the normality of his job as Archdeacon of Brecon and to pursue his own private ambitions. These latter were, of course, at the end of his journey predicated on his going on the Crusade.

He tells us that they started up a rough and narrow place called Malplace which led over Wenlock Edge. This route must have been along the line of the present country road between Caer Caradog to the south and the Lawley to the north. They did not pass through Wenlock itself, which was the home of St Milburge, whose church in Wenlock was destroyed many times. However, Pennant tells us that in 1101, when the church was being re-erected, 'a certain boy running hastily over the pavement, the vault of her sepulchre broke in under him, by which means the body of the holy virgin was discovered; which being taken up, an odoriferous exhalation, as of a most precious balsom, perfumed the whole church', followed by the inevitable glut of miracles. One assumes that the 'odoriferous' in this case means 'truly pleasant'.

Gerald tells us of a pun concerning Malplace. This concerns the Archdeacon of Shrewsbury, whose name was Peche, and the Dean, who was called Daiville or De Eyville. A Jew who was travelling with the two luminaries from Shrewsbury heard the Archdeacon comment that his jurisdiction spread from Malplace to Malpas near

Shrewsbury. He thought about the names of the clergymen and stated that 'It would be a miracle, if his fate brought him safely out of a country, whose archdeacon was sin, whose dean the devil; the entrance to the archdeaconry Ill-street, and its exit Bad-pass'!

The road over Wenlock Edge is surrounded by pleasant countryside and is nothing like as difficult as the journey must have been in 1188. The road they followed would have been down the Hope vale. In fact, on first sight it seems surprising that they did not take the route down what is now the road from Church Stretton and Craven Arms to Ludlow. On consideration the route over the hills is probably more direct. Had they taken the modern road they would have passed the settlement at Stokesay. Stokesay was mentioned in the Domesday Book and the land was given by Roger de Montgomery to Roger de Lacy, who in his turn leased some of the land to Theoderic de Say at South Stoke. The combination of the family name and Stoke produced the name Stokesay. The castle at Stokesay is a good example of a fortified merchant's dwelling, or manor house, the building of which commenced around 1281 and was completed within about ten years.

The money for the construction came out of wool dealing. Much of the wealth of England at the time stemmed from wool, and Stokesay is a reminder of how profitable and how important the wool trade was. The castle is a fine combination of stone defensive buildings coupled with timber-framed Elizabethan additions.

Nearby there is a small church which existed in the twelfth century, but sadly most was destroyed during the Civil War. It is probable that the present nave lies on the same line as the original one and the south door shows part of the Norman influence. There are some interesting box pews.

The road Gerald took goes past Bromfield which, as he mentions, hosted a little priory. This was built on ground between the confluence of the rivers Teme and Onny. It was probably founded in 900 and was certainly in existence in the reign of Edward the Confessor (1042–1066). In 1155 it was affiliated to the Benedictine abbey at Gloucester, thus becoming a Benedictine house. In the churchyard the remains of the original gatehouse are still visible and have been incorporated into a house. Part of the old boundary walls of the abbey can still be traced.

As for the church itself, there is still evidence of Norman building in the tower, even though it collapsed and needed to be rebuilt in about 1200, and the arches in the north and east walls of the chancel remain, implying that the original shape was a cruciform. But, despite the obvious attractions of Bromfield, Gerald tells us that they pressed on, coming next to Ludlow and its imposing castle.

Ludlow castle is bordered by the rivers Teme and Corve and holds a strong defensive position. Its existence is chronicled in 1138 but it goes back earlier than that. Obviously from Gerald's comments it was, in his day, a very powerful place and much of the structure now still visible, would have been in existence. It was built by the de Lacy family and was one of the Welsh border strongholds, a power base from which the Irish conquests were launched in 1171 under Hugh de Lacy. The Outer Bailey itself was of sufficient size for an army to be mustered there before the invasion of Ireland. The whole castle, including the Outer Bailey, covers a substantial area. This sheer size and magnificence would have been a factor in its becoming a palace as it was royal property from 1461 for over 300 years. It is now the property of the Earls of Powis.

In the inner bailey stands the Chapel of St Mary Magdalene, which has a circular chancel and a rectangular nave. The round nave is unusual and is said to have been based on the Church of the Holy Sepulchre in Jerusalem which had been erected in Jerusalem in 1048 on the site of Christ's tomb, and which would have been copied by the knights returning from the first Crusade.

St Mary's chapel, Ludlow

Another example of this is the Temple Church in London; otherwise, very few circular naves remain. The history connected to the castle is boundless, particularly in the sixteenth and seventeenth centuries, but as Gerald passed the castle by in his haste there is no time for lingering further. However, it should be stated that there are several beautiful buildings in the town dating back to the fifteenth century, including several timbered inns from then and the sixteenth century, recalling the wealth of the town.

At one end of the market square opposite to the castle itself and down some narrow lanes stands the impressive church of St Lawrence, topped by a magnificent mid fifteenth-century tower. Whilst the church was mostly rebuilt in the 1400s there are also remnants of the earlier rebuilding in 1199–1200 of an even earlier Norman church. There are some fascinating historial aspects of the church, not least that the heart of Prince Arthur, Henry VII's son, is buried here. He died on 2 April 1502; his body was transferred to Worcester cathedral.

Thence to Leominster. Leominster is yet another town which dates back to Anglo-Saxon times. Its church was founded in about 660. The manor of Leominster was referred to in the Domesday book, whilst the church was incorporated into the nave of the Benedictine Priory in about 1123. The borough of Leominster was founded shortly after that date. The only other Priory building which survives to this day, despite the ravages of the Dissolution, is the Priory House which may have housed the infirmary of the priory or, as the present day name implies, the prior himself. The priory of Leominster was refounded by Henry I in 1121 as a cell of Reading abbey, which was itself a Cluniac house. It remained a subsidiary of Reading despite its growing size and wealth.

The priory church itself is interesting inasmuch as it served two separate purposes in the Middle Ages. One of its functions was to be used as the priory church and the other function was as the parochial church. At the dissolution the monastic church was effectively destroyed. Nevertheless, the Romanesque carvings and parts of the surviving Norman architecture are worth inspection.

Then Gerald and Baldwin moved on to Hereford, leaving Maelienydd and Elfael, two of the cantrefs of Wales, on their right hand side.

It must have been a huge relief that after having ridden a long way in the day through the countryside, they dropped down a hill to the plain where Hereford stands, with the huge edifice of the cathedral clearly visible above the city. It must have seemed like heaven to our very weary travellers. Gerald himself comments that they had described a full circle and returned to where they had begun 'this rather exhausting journey through Wales'. He states that, as has been evident through the history of the journey, they had all worked very hard to make the journey very successful. They had recruited about 3,000 men to the cross, all experienced men highly skilled in the use of spears and arrows and, according to Gerald, all ready and keen to get on with the Crusade. However, he says that if only the Crusade could be carried out with such enthusiasm as they had engendered throughout their journey, it could only be a great success.

In fact the Third Crusade was a political disaster. The main combatants fell out. According to Gerald, the aged Holy Roman Emperor Frederick Barbarosa delayed the Crusade because he was of a dilatory nature. However, history has shown that he revealed great leadership, certainly in the early stages of his German armies' passage through Hungary, and it was largely his willpower which had held his army together. Then, hardly his fault, he was drowned in Cilicia on 10 June 1190, after which much of his army drifted away.

Henry I of England and Philip II of France had been very keen on the Crusade and worked together but Henry died, leaving the task to his successor Richard I, who took up the strain. Strain it was, as there was much dissension between Richard and Philip II. Richard's fleet was hit by heavy storms and suffered much loss. To recover he stopped on Cyprus on his way to the Holy Land. He fell out with Isaac, Dukas Comnaris of Cyprus, who not only seized much of Richard's treasure and refused to give it back, but also suspended the laws of hospitality to Richard. Richard therefore had no option but to take over Cyprus by force of arms. Then the King of Sicily, another major player, who supplied much of the provisions for the Crusaders, died in 1189. This combination of events was hardly promising.

When Acre fell in 1191 there were many quarrels

amongst the Crusaders as to how the spoils were to be shared. The rest of the Third Crusade was a dismal failure inasmuch as the Crusaders did not achieve their objective to regain Jerusalem. However, Richard did obtain a treaty, which meant that, although Saladin continued in his total control of Jerusalem, he agreed to the minor concession of allowing unarmed Christians to access the city. The Crusaders withdrew, and it was left to the Fourth Crusade to rectify the position – but this, too, was a disaster and Jerusalem remained in Muslim hands.

The Crusade was also a personal disaster for Baldwin, as he lost his life in the battle for Acre. This was a sad end to all his enthusiastic recruitment around Wales. Gerald, however, is philosophical about all this, saying: 'These things are allowed to happen, since adversity tempers our understanding and we gain strength from our very weakness' – or, we should learn from our mistakes.

Chapter 27
Baldwin, Archbishop of Canterbury, and Gerald, Archdeacon of Brecon

At the end of the road Gerald decides to tell us about Archbishop Baldwin who had been living with him in close contact for the last seven weeks around Wales. Some of his traits we have already seen but it is better to use Gerald's words to describe him as, after all, he must have known him well by now:

> He was a man of dark complexion, of an open and venerable countenance, of a moderate stature, a good person, and rather inclined to be thin rather than corpulent. He was a modest and grave man, of so real abstinence and continence, that ill report scarcely ever presumed to say any thing against him; a man of few words; slow to anger, temperate and moderate in all his passions and affections; swift to hear, slow to speak.
>
> He was brought up in the church from an early age and embraced the religious life and assumed with holy devotion the habit of the Cistercian order; and as he had been formerly more than a monk in his manners, within the space of a year he was appointed abbot, and in a few years afterwards preferred first to a bishopric, and then to an archbishopric; . . . So great was his lenity that he put an end to all pastoral rigour and was a better monk than an abbot, a better bishop than an archbishop. Hence Pope Urban addressed him: 'Urban, servant of the servants of God, to the most fervent monk, to the warm abbot, to the luke-warm bishop, to the remiss archbishop, health &c &c.

It is a fairly damning indictment of a good man promoted above his station, and it has been seen that Baldwin did have some humour and must also have had both significant stamina and courage in delivering his mission. Given that so many were prevailed upon to take the cross he must have had a good way with words and preached convincingly in what must have been a most difficult and daunting mission for an English archbishop, in what must have seemed to him to be a foreign land.

Equally he and Gerald must have spoken long and frequently about all sorts of matters. In *Gemma Ecclesiastica* Gerald relates a story of extraordinary temptation which had been told to him, presumably during their journey together, by 'The holy and venerable Baldwin, archbishop of Canterbury'. It concerns the temptation of a clergyman by a gorgeous lady who tries and nearly seduces him. Finally he says that if she would take communion on Easter Sunday he would succumb to her blandishments. She does, and follows him out looking even more voluptuous than hitherto. He still isn't too sure that it is quite right when they 'indulge in licentious kisses and embraces, bent upon complete satisfaction of her lust.' So he calls over her dog, a greyhound bitch, called Galiena and played with it, much to the jealous wrath of the girl. She is furious that he has neglected her for her dog and effectively curses him, saying that they will never meet again. Soon after he falls head over heels with a girl called Galiena and is spurned. He tries, but gets nowhere, and eventually takes vows and enters a Cistercian house to escape temptation. It does no good, so he tells the abbot, who consults the bishop, and he confesses before the whole chapter of monks. It was decided that they all should say prayers for their brother, and indeed the prayers should be said by the Order throughout the world. The prayers didn't work and so, shortly after, he died unrelieved and afflicted in spirit. Gerald's view is that the woman was a mere apparition, although it is amazing that she (or it) could take communion and could determine a means to revenge:

> There is no doubt that the apparition only knew as much as Divine Providence permitted it to know, and no more. Such a grave temptation and persecution, in truth, was divinely inflicted [on the cleric] either as a punishment or as a purification, that is, to punish his sins committed previously or to increase his good merits (as was the case with Job and Tobias) if he would persevere.

So obviously Baldwin and Gerald must have discussed many things and they also had the subtle ability of turning a story into a moral tale!

Gerald at work

One wonders whether Gerald was entirely independent in his assessment of Baldwin bearing in mind his ambition to be Bishop of St David's. Maybe he did not feel he had Baldwin's full backing for the post, notwithstanding his close attention to Baldwin right round Wales. His final words concerning Baldwin was that he, to the end of his life before Acre, helped and encouraged those around him, giving presents and gifts and overall involving them in a selfless Christian charity.

Gerald has been the centrepiece of the journey both as its central character and its scribe. Reaching back over the years we have learnt much about him. He was a godly man and a fairly strict disciplinarian who wished to clean up some of the problems of the church, exemplified by his comments regarding the state of Llanthony and the peculiar practices of Llanbadarn, and also his guidance to the clergy through his *Gemma Ecclesiastica*. He was full of reforming zeal. He was a witty man and must have been good company on the road in the long winter evenings of their journey. He was a good preacher, although it is mainly he who tells us this, and could speak in several languages, including, of course, Welsh, and acted as an interpreter to Baldwin at various stages. He was clearly a good administrator and one imagines that he must have been involved to some degree in much of the planning of the journey. He was also tough in his approach if he felt he was being wronged, as Bishop Adam of St Asaph had found out. Probably he was mainly responsible for keeping the party moving despite the problems and hazards of the road. But then he knew and was known to most of the Welsh princes and, in particular, was related to Lord Rhys. In fact he seems to have known and to have been known by most of the kings of England, too, during his life, and many of those in power and with influence in both Wales and England, and even with the

Popes in Rome.

He was apparently tall and handsome in his early years and must have been quite a formidable figure. He did not suffer fools gladly and was pretty outspoken about Baldwin and others including de Broase and even Lord Rhys, but he seems to have survived politically despite his sharp or ironic tongue. Overall he was well aware of his abilities and his ambition, which, as we have seen, he wore on his sleeve. He must have given his many mentors considerable problems over the years as he obstinately stuck to his guns in seeking to attain his aims.

In fact many of the things he did could be seen within the context of Gerald seeking to achieve the see of St David's. This even includes his book, and the dedication to Stephen Langton, Archbishop of Canterbury between 1207 and 1208, as he seeks to put himself, not unnaturally, in a good light administratively, spiritually and temporally throughout his writing. In a way it is a pretty formidable curriculum vitae!

Even in the preface he made his point, as when he appealed to Archbishop Stephen Langton's common sense. He wrote:

> [You] who unmindful of worldly affections, do not partially distribute your bounties to your family and friends, but to letters and merit; you, who in the midst of such great and unceasing contests between the crown and the priesthood, stand forth almost singly the firm and faithful friend of the British church; you, who, almost the only one duly elected, fulfil the scriptural designation of the Episcopal character . . .

In other words: Stephen, you know I have followed all the rules just like you, so how about getting on with my appointment to St David's? Gerald was descended both from the Marcher lords and the Welsh princes. He could also be tough and ironic. Bearing in mind his love of Wales he wrote sarcastically to Archbishop Walter the Chief Justiciary, who had just defeated the Welsh on land between the Wye and the Severn, 'Blessed be to God who has taught your hands to war and your fingers to fight, for since the days when Harold almost exterminated the nation, no prince has destroyed so many Welshmen in one Battle as your Grace' (Little). Problems of dual nationality may nevertheless have hampered his ambitions, as he was neither wholly in the Norman camp or the Welsh camp. Sadly, Gerald's main attributes were also his Achilles heel, but his determination throughout his life to attain independence of the Welsh church from subservience to the English Archbishop of Canterbury, albeit still owing allegiance to Rome, shows where his heart truly lay.

Gerald had always sought to become the Bishop of St David's in what he regarded as the metropolitan see of Wales. He reminds us that St David's was once the metropolitan city of an archbishop, not just a bishop, and also capital of Wales. His belief for this relies on some myths and a certain amount of fictional and wishful thinking. But, there is no doubt that Gerald's ambition had always been to follow in the footsteps of his uncle David FitzGerald, Bishop of St David's, who died in 1176. Gerald hoped that, as bishop, he would be able to sever St David's subservience to Canterbury, and then be directly responsible as bishop for the country of Wales to the Pope in Rome. He even hoped for the Pope to give him the 'pallium', thereby making him Archbishop. He was to come close to his wish several times for, after the death of this uncle, the canons of St David's met together to put forward names of candidates to King Henry II to choose from. The Chapter recommended the names of the four archdeacons, of whom Gerald was one. In fact it was rumoured that Gerald was the only name recommended, but in the event all the names were sent off for adjudication. When the case came before the king, all the bishops and the then Archbishop of Canterbury, Richard, 'spoke in favour of Gerald, lauding his reforming zeal and his physical courage, stressing his scholarship, and speaking at length of his noble birth and his kinship with Rhys ap Gruffudd, Prince of South Wales, and with so many other high-born Welshmen' (Thorpe). It would seem that Gerald was on to a sure thing and that he was the obvious choice for preferment. However, the king was aware of Gerald's ambitions and his wish to cease subservience to Canterbury. He would clearly have had a very fresh memory of the death of Thomas à Becket less than six years before and the king's part in it, however inadvertent. Even so he also would have been very alive to the political problems of two independent archbishops, both within the same kingdom, reporting to Rome, and the effect on his own influence.

So, sadly for Gerald, as we have seen, the king appointed the then Cluniac Prior of Much Wenlock in Shropshire, Peter de Leia, as Bishop. He was an Anglo-Norman by birth, and a person much more likely to be compliant with the king. (Gerald, we recall, was descended both from the Marcher lords and the Welsh princes.)

Gerald's quest for a bishopric was not over. He was offered the Bishopric of Bangor in the 1190s, which he refused. Prince John offered him the Bishopric of Llandaff, which he again refused, as only that of St David's was the preferment he sought. He also had been offered a bishopric twice in Ireland, again refused by him. He must have been regarded as a person difficult to please even though his ambitions were remarkably consistent. In 1198 de Leia died and Gerald attempted again to attain his prize, this time with a five-year battle, which he fought tenaciously. He was still determined to free the church in Wales from the yoke of Canterbury, even if he had to die in his chancel as had Thomas à Becket before him. He still had many powerful friends in Wales and was well equipped both politically and religiously for the post. But strangely, just because he was so well favoured and politically adept, this may well have not acted in his favour as his connections made him too powerful and too dangerous a man to replace de Leia. He was in modern parlance 'over-qualified' for the post.

In 1198 a similar pattern to the previous election was followed, with the Chapter sending four alternatives to Hubert Walter, then Archbishop of Canterbury, with Gerald heading the list. Hubert would not accept the list and offered two of his own candidates who were both refused. Subsequently King Richard I summoned to his presence four members of the Chapter, but his letter requesting their attendance was delayed. Because of this delay the canons went instead to Lincoln where they talked with Gerald and subsequently refused two new potential candidates, and sent news to King Richard of that fact. King Richard died in 1199 so the decision passed on to King John. The selection started all over again! King John seems to have been pro-Gerald. He wrote both to Gerald in Lincoln and to the chapter at St David's telling them of his favourable view. Gerald's spirits must have risen at this news as it would have seemed he was at last nearing his ambition. However, John informed the Justiciar to do nothing about the appointment until he, John, had seen Gerald. John was crowned in 1199 and informed Gerald along with two of the Chapter that he was minded to accept him as bishop. But he then postponed the appointment as the Archbishop of Canterbury was against Gerald's holding the office. Gerald went to St David's and was elected by the whole Chapter as bishop and was directed by them to go to Rome to be consecrated by the Pope and thus achieve the separation from Canterbury together with some finality to the appointment process. All this had taken nearly a year and at last it seemed as if he had made it!

But alas another four and a half years of struggle were ahead. The Archbishop of Canterbury and the Justiciar were not going to be pushed to one side and wrote to the Chapter telling them to appoint Geoffrey de Henelawe, Prior of Llanthony. The Chapter appealed to the Pope and off Gerald went to Rome to meet Pope Innocent III. There he was to learn of the Pope's great art of procrastination which was far greater and subtler than that of the English kings. Nothing was resolved between the years 1199 to 1203. Needless to say everyone, including the Chapter of St David's, was becoming thoroughly fed up with the whole process. Gerald started to return to St David's in 1203 but was thrown into prison at Chatillon-sur-Seine at the tender age of sixty! The following night he was freed and carried on his journey north and after a further journey came before King John at Elboeuf, near Rouen, for a long awaited meeting. Gerald protested about the possible election of three other contenders 'on the grounds that the first was practically illiterate, the second a bastard and the third a notorious fornicator.' Obviously all good reasons for appointment! He further appealed to the Bishop of Lincoln and to the Archbishop of Canterbury.

The last episode in the saga was when Hubert Walter the Archbishop and the Justiciar Geoffey FitzPeter called the canons of St David's and Gerald to Westminster, Gerald having had a preliminary talk with Hubert Walter at Waltham abbey. They announced the new Bishop of St David's to be Geoffrey, the man they had selected some five years before. Gerald, presumably briefed at Waltham, accepted the news without a murmur. At the same time he resigned, one assumes with great sadness, from his archdeaconry of Brecon and the Prebend of Mathry. It must have been a very poignant moment to see all his dreams vanish, but he had been always resolute and even obstinate in his views. If he could not achieve his ambition of the episcopate, without being subservient to Canterbury, so be it. Most of the above story is told us by Gerald himself in *De iure et statu Menevius Ecclesia* ('The rites and privileges of the Church of St David's') and is thus, no doubt, somewhat biased in his favour. Nevertheless it gives a picture of a man with an overwhelming mission but who was sufficiently a man at peace with himself to be able to accept the final verdict with dignity and humility. It also is an interesting commentary on the contemporary politics of the appointment of a Bishop and the conflict between church and State, even in Gerald's time. Perhaps this is echoed in the present time, although the participants and systems are somewhat different.

However well Gerald took his fate, when one looks back at the buildings and church of the time one wonders whether he was seduced, to some degree at least, by the prospect of the power and wealth which the appointment to the bishopric brought with it. A twelfth-century bishop was imbued with a near kingly status with both temporal and spiritual influence. The church had the power to influence kings themselves, although the fate of Thomas à Becket was a warning to clergy not to stray too far into the wrong domain. Perhaps these thoughts are unfair as Gerald was regarded as a reformer and administrator and a good and godly man and no doubt he would have made a good and godly Bishop of Wales. Emphasising these qualities he is not loath to criticise the mother church in the time of Henry I as being renowned for both its wealth and its religious practices which he sarcastically points out are 'two things which you rarely find united'. He is scathing about the Benedictine Order saying that whilst, in its original vows of poverty, it was admirable, it had in his day accumulated great wealth through many benefactors 'with the result that under cover of a most regrettable dispensation, gluttony and indulgence ended in corruption'. He draws from the classical writers such as Seneca and Ovid, quoting the latter as saying, 'Our wealth has grown so great and yet our greed grows greater: however much we have, still more we'll covet later'. Nevertheless his ambition was deep as was his involvement with nearly everyone worth knowing in royal as well as religious circles, including kings and popes; and if not wealth, the power an ecclesiastical appointment brings must have played some part in his thinking.

Our journey is complete, but that of Gerald carried on some thirty-five years. He died in 1223 at the age of nearly eighty. Despite the great glories of his life he passed his final days in humble circumstances, albeit amongst his books, 'confessing his sins in the dim recesses of churches'. He was a sad figure at his end but his works have survived 800 years. So, in the end, perhaps his true ambitions to find a place in history were achieved and his spirit remains with us encapsulated in 'his difficult mission to Wales'.

The final words of this book should be those of Gerald himself as he set out what he hoped to achieve in his writing:

> Lest my pen should be injured by the rust of idleness, I have throught good to commit to writing the devout visitation which Baldwin Archbishop of Canterbury made throughout Wales; and to hand down, as it were in a mirror, through you, O illustrious Stephen, to posterity, the difficult places through which we passed, the names of springs and torrents, the witty

sayings, the toils and incidents of the journey, the memorable events of ancient and modern times, and the natural history and description of the country; lest my study should perish through idleness, or the praise of these things be lost by my silence.

Bibliography

Adam of Usk, ed. Sir Edward Maunde Thompson, *The Chronicle of Adam of Usk* (Llanerch Enterprises, 1990)

A tour through the South of England, Wales and part of Ireland (Minerva Press, London, 1843)

Martin Aurell, *Geoffrey of Monmouth's History and the Twelfth-Century Renaissance* (Haskins Society Journal 18, Woodbridge and Rochester, 2007)

Mikhail Baktin, *Rabelais and his World* (University Press, Indiana, 1984)

Chris Barber, *More Mysterious Wales* (Grafton Books, London, 1987)

Joanna Billing, *The hidden places of Wales* (Travel Publishing, 2004)

William Bingley, *The Rev., North Wales* (Bryer, London, 1814)

T. D. Breverton, *The Book of Welsh Saints* (Glyndŵr Publishing, Cowgate, 2000)

CADW, *A Mirror of Medieval Wales: Gerald and his Journey of 1188* (Cardiff, 1988)

Nicholas Crane, *Great British Journeys* (Weidenfeld & Nicholson, London, 2008)

O. E. Craster, *Llanthony Priory* (HMSO, Edinburgh)

J. Evans, The Rev., *Letters written during a tour through South Wales in the year 1803 and at other Times* (Baldwin, London, 1804)

Exhibition on Tartar (Azjatycka Gallery, Warsaw, 1997)

Gerald of Wales, *The Journey through Wales/The description of Wales* (trans. Lewis Thorpe), (Penguin, 1978)

Gerald of Wales, *Jewel of the Church* (trans. John J. Hagen) (Brill, Leide, 1979)

Geraldus de Barri, *The Itinerary of Archbishop Baldwin through Wales* (trans. Sir Richard Colt Hoare Bart.) (William Miller, London, 1806), 2 volumes

Elissa R. Henkin, *Traditions of the Welsh Saints* (Boydell and Brewer, Woodbridge and Wolfeboro, 1987)

Sir Richard Colt Hoare, *The Journeys of Sir Richard Colt Hoare through Wales and England*, 1793–1810, ed. M. W. Thompson (Alan Sutton, Gloucester, 1973)

Norman Housley, *Fighting for the Cross* (Yale University Press, New Haven and London, 2008)

Simon Jenkins, *Wales churches, houses, castles* (Alan Lane, Penguin Books, London, 2008)

Julie Kerr, *Food, Drink and Lodging: Hospitality in Twelfth-Century England* (Haskins Society Journal 18, Woodbridge and Rochester, 2007)

Francis Kilvert, The Rev., *Kilvert's Diaries* (ed. William Plomer) (Jonathan Cape, London, 1977), 3 volumes

John Leland, *Itinerary in England and Wales* (ed. Lucy Toulmin Smith) (Centaur Press, London, 1964), 5 volumes

W. J. Lewis, *A History of Lampeter* (Sir Ceredigion County Council, 1997)

A. G. Little, *Medieval Wales* (T. Fisher Unwin, London, 1902)

Ian Mortimer, *The Time Traveller's Guide to Medieval England* (Vintage, London, 1970)

Andrew Morton, *Trees of the Celtic Saints: the Ancient Yews of Wales* (Carreg Gwalch, 2009)

T. Pennant (abr. D. Kirk), *A Tour in Wales* (Carreg Gwalch, 1998)

Jonathan Phillips, *The Fourth Crusade and the Sack of Constantinople* (Pimlico, 2005)

Byron Rogers, *The Bank Manager and the Holy Grail* (Aurum Press, London, 2003)

Christian Saunders, *Into the Dragon's Lair* (Carreg Gwalch, 2003)

R. V. Tooley, *Maps and Map-maker* (Batsford, London, 1970)

John Walker, *Vernacular Architecture 30* (1999)

Frank Ward, *The Lakes of Wales* (Herbert Jenkins, London, 1931)

E. M. Wilkie, *Legends of Welsh Saints* (SPCK, London, 1947)

Various and many church guides, CADW booklets, and internet pages

Heritage

Visit our website for further information:

www.carreg-gwalch.com

Orders can be placed on our

On-line Shop

Photography and Text

Visit our website for further information:
www.carreg-gwalch.com
Orders can be placed on our
On-line Shop